SOUTH AFRICA

DILEMMAS IN WORLD POLITICS

Series Editor
George A. Lopez, University of Notre Dame

Dilemmas in World Politics offers teachers and students of international relations a series of quality books on critical issues, trends, and regions in international politics. Each text will examine a "real world" dilemma and will be structured to cover the historical, theoretical, practical, and projected dimensions of its subject.

EDITORIAL BOARD

BOOKS IN THIS SERIES

SOUTH AFRICA

■ ■ ■

Domestic Crisis
and Global Challenge

Kenneth W. Grundy
Case Western Reserve University

Westview Press
BOULDER □ SAN FRANCISCO □ OXFORD

Dilemmas in World Politics Series

Internal design by Libby Barstow. Cover design by Polly Christensen.

Published in 1991 in the United States of America by Westview Press, Inc., 5500 Central Avenue, Boulder, Colorado 80301, and in the United Kingdom by Westview Press, 36 Lonsdale Road, Summertown, Oxford OX2 7EW

Library of Congress Cataloging-in-Publication Data
Grundy, Kenneth W.
  South Africa : domestic crisis and global challenge / Kenneth W.
Grundy.
    p.   cm. — (Dilemmas in world politics)
  Includes bibliographical references and index.
  ISBN 0-8133-0910-7 — ISBN 0-8133-0911-5 (paperback)
  1. South Africa—Politics and government—1948–   .   2. South Africa—
Foreign relations.   3. South Africa—Politics and government—
Foreign public opinion.   4. Apartheid—South Africa.   I. Title.
II. Series.
DT1938.G78   1991
968.06—dc20   91-12686
                                                                                      CIP

Printed and bound in the United States of America

The paper used in this publication meets the requirements of the American National Standard for Permanence of Paper for Printed Library Materials Z39.48-1984.

10   9   8   7   6   5   4   3   2   1

Dedicated to
those South Africans
whose higher vision accepts nothing less
than justice for all

□ □ □

Contents

□ □ □

Preface

South Africa is just one state in a world of more than 164 sovereign states. Its system of race relations, known as apartheid, features a mode of governance in which a mere 14 percent of the population, the white minority, controls and makes authoritative decisions for the entire country. That fact, in itself, speaks volumes about the absence of democracy in South Africa. But the situation is worse still.

Not all whites share the aims of the ruling National Party (NP). In the 1989 general election, the NP captured only 48 percent of the white vote. The total votes for this NP government represent the preferences of only 6 percent of the adult population of South Africa. Nonetheless, because the NP directs government policy, it exercises inordinate power in its efforts to establish the pattern of rule and the pace of change.

Of course, South Africa is not the only undemocratic government in the world, and it is certainly not the most violent or repressive one. Proportionately far more people have died as a result of political violence in Burundi, Rwanda, Sri Lanka, Somalia, Ethiopia, Lebanon, El Salvador, Uganda, and Cambodia. Inefficiency and corruption are more deep-seated and openly exhibited elsewhere. Similarly, there are fewer political prisoners in South Africa than in dozens of other states. The government in Pretoria, for all its selfish interests, pays more attention to the material and social needs of its unrepresented citizenry than do the governments of numerous other states, including some of South Africa's most vocal critics. For example, earlier regimes in Equatorial Guinea, Ethiopia, Uganda, Burundi, the Central African Republic, Romania, Paraguay, Cambodia (Kampuchea), and Haiti as well as the current regimes in Ethiopia, Somalia, the Sudan, Iraq, Mauritania and Burma (Myanmar) make a mockery of the concepts of popular and representative government.

Yet South Africa is regarded, in the words of a progovernment newspaper, as the "polecat of the world." Others call it a pariah, a lightning rod, an evil system, even a Nazi or a fascist state; and they insist that South Africa should be rejected or isolated from the world community or, worse, that it should be a target of the world's collective political and even military energies until a nonracial government is installed in power there.

Why has South Africa's domestic order created such a furor around the world? Why do apartheid and the policies designed to defend racial superordination arouse emotions far from South Africa's borders? Why did South Africa become a major issue in foreign affairs, whereas the systematic massacre of more than 1 million Kampucheans from 1975 to 1979 did little more than stir passing interest and inspire an award-winning film, *The Killing Fields* (1985)? South Africa has been on the agenda of the United Nations and other international organizations since 1947. Other repressive systems manage to avoid the gaze of all but specialists and committed activists. The persistent sins of those systems light candles of interest that soon fizzle and burn low.

Thus, it is the question "Why South Africa?" that provides the motive for this book. What is so important about South Africa that makes Americans and Europeans as well as Africans take such a keen interest in what happens there? To answer these questions, we must examine apartheid not only as a domestic South African phenomenon but also as an international affairs issue. And we must place apartheid in its historical context. These discussions will enable us to explore the various ways in which individuals, groups, governments, and groups of governments can address the realities of apartheid. Together these shall inform our discussion of what can and ought to be done about apartheid in South Africa and with what potential effects.

The difficulty for policymakers—the fact that South Africa does not constitute a fixed target—is precisely what makes the country such an exciting case in international politics today. Its government and both the supporters and the opponents of apartheid are continually changing their policies and strategies. This fluidity makes it especially difficult to fashion common policies among foreign governments that want to bring about a relatively smooth transition to majority rule. It also complicates the task of coalition building in South Africa itself. That is why South African politics sometimes takes on a free-for-all character, with occasional surprise turns. It is into this dynamic and transitional setting that we shall now plunge, aware that the rich and complex diversity of South African society can be lost in the quest for patterns, trends, and commonalities.

Kenneth W. Grundy

□ □ □

Acronyms

ANC	African National Congress
AWB	Afrikaner Weerstandsbeweging
BERI	Business Environment Risk Index
CYL	Congress Youth League
EPG	Eminent Persons Group
IAEA	International Atomic Energy Agency
ICU	Industrial and Commercial Workers' Union
JMCs	Joint Management Centres
MNCs	multinational corporations
MPLA	Movimento Popular de Libertação de Angola
NATO	North Atlantic Treaty Organization
NGOs	nongovernmental organizations
NICs	newly industrialized countries
NP	National Party
NPT	Non-Proliferation Treaty
NSMS	National Security Management System
NSSM	National Security Study Memorandum
OAU	Organization of African Unity
PAC	Pan Africanist Congress
RSA	Republic of South Africa
SACP	South African Communist Party
SADCC	Southern African Development Coordination Conference
SADF	South African Defense Force
SANROC	South African Non-Racial Olympic Committee
SAP	South African Police
SASO	South African Students' Organization
SWAPO	South West African People's Organization
UDF	United Democratic Front
UN	United Nations
UNESCO	United Nations Educational, Scientific, and Cultural Organization
UNITA	União Nacional para la Independência Total de Angola

UPU	Universal Postal Union
WCC	World Council of Churches
WHO	World Health Organization
ZANU	Zimbabwe African National Union
ZAPU	Zimbabwe African People's Union

Southern Africa

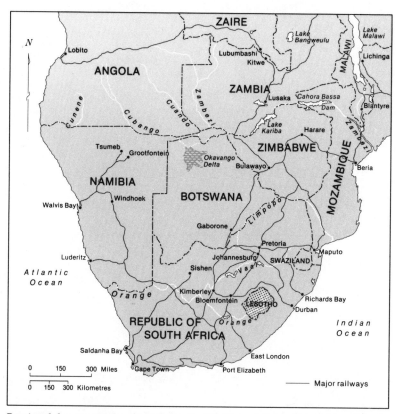

Reprinted by permission from John E. Bardill and James H. Cobbe, *Lesotho: Dilemmas of Dependence in Southern Africa* (Boulder, Colo.: Westview Press, 1985).

ONE

□ □ □

What Is So Important About South Africa?

[A]partheid is *the* operative term in South Africa. From apartheid and the effort to implement and maintain it flow South Africa's domestic, social, economic, and political systems. The resistance to apartheid provides the framework for contemporary progressive politics in that land. So, too, does apartheid affect the foreign policy of South Africa, in terms of both the way foreign states treat Pretoria (South Africa's administrative capital) and the way Pretoria deals with outsiders, especially the countries of neighboring southern Africa.

Apartheid is indeed the chief cause of South Africa's problems; it is the evil that must be rooted out. But we cannot assume that the struggle by South Africans will be won once apartheid has been ended. Even as the legal basis for apartheid is being amended and dismantled before our eyes, pervasive poverty—to a large extent compounded by apartheid and distributed chiefly among Black South Africans—will continue to bedevil governments and other social institutions and organizations.[1] Ending apartheid will not automatically end poverty. The struggle for both social justice and economic security must not be abandoned. Let us begin the chapter by recounting the story of one South African family.

A BRIEF PRIMER ON APARTHEID

Nozukile lives in the Transkei, an ostensibly "independent" homeland (*bantustan*).[2] She has been married twenty years. For eighteen of those years her husband, Ntoyi, has been working and living in Cape Town,

650 miles away. He visits his home just two weeks a year. He has had five years of schooling; she has never been to school. He does contract work (with thirteen different jobs in those twenty years), and his salary, now 525 rand (R) per month (the equivalent of about 200 U.S. dollars), enables him to send R50 a month to his wife. This is her only source of income, except for what she can earn from keeping two dozen chickens and three cattle, and from tending the garden of her husband's elder brother. As the brother is away working too, Nozukile stays with his wife because Ntoyi has no farm plot of his own.

Off and on Nozukile has been to Cape Town, staying first in Nyanga, a Black township, and then in a wood and plastic shelter at Crossroads, a squatter settlement on the Cape Flats. Some of her stays have been extended two or three years at a time. She misses her husband. She especially suffered while raising their five children (two others died in infancy in part because the healthcare facilities were forty miles away). The two eldest boys need the guidance and encouragement of their father in these troubled times. One has already been arrested several times for his political activities at school. Nozukile would have stayed longer in Cape Town except she knew that she would never be able to secure their claim to land in the Transkei if she was away from the homeland. Equally important, she was forced on one occasion to abandon her shack at Crossroads when government bulldozers smashed it. She had been there in violation of diverse laws designed to limit the influx of Blacks into "white" urban areas. After they rebuilt their shack, it was burnt down by the *Witdoeke*, Black vigilantes who enjoy police protection.

The majority of men in Crossroads are legally in the Cape; that is, they have proper work permits and hence may look for housing there. But most of the women and children were not supposed to leave their homeland without the proper endorsements from local chiefs and labor officers. They had to carry their passbooks, internal passports that every Black South African was required to produce on demand. Without permissions in the passbook, they were "illegal." Once Ntoyi was arrested and charged with "harboring" his wife. He successfully bribed the policeman to drop the charge.

But the problem grows worse. The Transkei is dry. Land is scarce. Full-time jobs are virtually nonexistent. It is estimated that one out of every three economically active males in the Transkei is unemployed. Underemployment—that is, employment at less than full time and full pay so that one is kept at a low standard of living—is just as high. Social services are also minimal. In short, there has been little, other than South African law, to keep people in the Transkei. Thus they drift to the cities, to East London, Port Elizabeth, and Cape Town, ashamed of their inferior legal and economic status, yet determined to find work and make a home. People in other homelands are drawn to other cities. Kwazulu services Durban; Bophuthatswana, Venda, and Lebowa, and other homelands service the Johannesburg and Pretoria region. The number of squatters in the Western Cape grew from 25,000 in 1978 to an estimated 400,000 in 1987. Indeed the migratory labor system is an integral part of the economy of apartheid.

In Crossroads, life is not secure. Overcrowding has reached inhuman levels. One survey revealed an average of 2.7 persons per room, 6.5 per bed, and 12.0 per nonflush toilet. Not until 1984 did the state concede the right of squatters to remain in Crossroads. Before that, and even afterward, shacks were demolished by the authorities. Police also regularly evicted "illegals." Even the meager social services provided in the permanent Black townships outside the white towns and cities are unavailable in the shanty towns. There is no electricity. Fuel is mostly wood collected by the people. Many squatters have tried to organize services for themselves, with the assistance of private relief agencies and church groups. In Crossroads the squatters built two schools and staffed them; organized adult literacy and home nursing programs; opened a clinic staffed by a volunteer doctor; arranged for counseling and legal aid services; and established refuse collection, a primitive sewage-disposal system, clubs, cooperative self-help schemes, shops, and other services. The informal economy and community spirit are amazing in the face of government harassment. The people are determined to seize control of their own lives. Eventually the government relented, albeit partially: It decided that Crossroads could stay, but that it must house only the original 25,000 inhabitants. The authorities did their best to remove the overflow, including the residents of the satellite camps that sprang up around Crossroads in the 1980s.

It was part of the government's scheme to exploit the ongoing political competition by Black politicians for control of Crossroads. The police encouraged and even secretly armed the more conservative faction. The result, however, was very bloody. In 1985 and 1986, Crossroads became a battlefield. It was practically burnt to the ground, and 70,000 people were made homeless. Approximately a hundred were killed. The state, determined to relocate large numbers of squatters, succeeded in turning Black against Black. Police, Defense Force, and *Witdoek* vigilantes worked together to destroy the community, which had been trying to upgrade itself. The fighting and looting achieved what government had not been able to in ten years of harassment: It cleared the area of people so that the upgrading of Crossroads could begin. The government offered alternative sites at Khayelitsha, but the people resisted the forced removals to a location so far from their work and friends.

In 1986, Nozukile returned to the Transkei for the last time. As of 1991, she and Ntoyi are separated again. But during his visits and in letters they discuss her return to the Cape (to Khayelitsha this time) and a permanent home. Now it is the terrible economic situation rather than the government's authority that poses the greatest challenge to their dreams.

No single story can describe Black South African life in all its rich variety, complexity and confusion. Hundreds of thousands of variations could be sketched on the theme represented by Nozukile's life situation. The omission of some details and the overemphasis on others should not be troubling. There are some circumstances that almost all South African Blacks have in common—powerlessness, vulnerability, economic insecurity, and a lack of fulfillment. But many also share a persistence and determination to change their lives. Perhaps it is for this reason that Nelson Mandela is such a powerful symbol to South Africa's Blacks. He represents hope precisely because he refused to compromise on his demand for unconditional release from prison, and he eventually got his way. In spite of all the degradation and poverty of South Africa, there is an optimism and faith among the Black people that transcends the physical and political setting. To be Black in South Africa is to be less than complete; hence political action is seen as the vehicle for change. Even economic tools—boycotts, strikes, stay-at-homes, and rent strikes—serve political purposes. The Black struggle for dignity and power is as much a product of apartheid as are the denigration and frustration that are apartheid's immediate manifestations.

Apartheid means literally "apartness." As a policy, it has been so discredited by the world community and by most South Africans that the government in Pretoria has sought to mask it, labeling it variously as "separate development," "parallel development," "multinational development," and "cooperative coexistence." More recently, various government officials have verbally rejected apartheid, declaring it "dead." They have pledged to end apartheid and to dismantle its laws and institutions. But many critics are convinced that Pretoria does not mean business.

Apartheid is the centerpiece of a society that thrives on the pervasive reality of race-based power and privilege and social super- and subordination. It is an elaborate theoretical rationalization for the racial domination that has prevailed in South Africa virtually since the first European settlers arrived at the Cape of Good Hope in 1652. It seeks to reconcile continued white rule during an era in which majoritarian democracy is the ideal in most of the Western world. Accordingly, apartheid's more sophisticated apologists forsake the open advocacy (at least among most white South Africans) of the idea of white supremacy.

Rather, since the NP government was established in 1948, the official focus has been not on the alleged inferiority or superiority of one race but on the differences between the races. By celebrating and encouraging racial differences and promoting ethnic divisions in the Black population, apartheid seeks to justify the creation of separate **homelands**—separate territories assigned for the exclusive use of each major Black nationality group. Thus the Tswana have the ostensibly independent homeland of Bophuthatswana, the Vhacenda have Venda, and the Xhosa have two homelands, the Ciskei and the Transkei. There are other homelands, not yet "independent" for one reason or another, for the Zulu (Kwazulu), Swazi (Kangwane), Southern Ndebele (Kwandebele), North Sotho (Lebowa), South Sotho (Qwa Qwa), and the Machangana-Songa (Gazankulu). But homelands have not been created (or even suggested) for either the Indian people or the so-called Coloureds (of mixed race), who have been legally disadvantaged in other ways as well.

This is not the place to argue the supposed merits of the homeland scheme from Pretoria's standpoint. Suffice to say that the territory allocated for the homelands is some 13 percent of South Africa's total land area, a percentage meant to accommodate nearly three-quarters of the entire population. Many homelands consist of several noncontiguous parcels of relatively unproductive territory with little in the way of resources, infrastructure, arable land, or viable industries, towns, and cities. Nozukile's struggle to survive in the Transkei is thus not unusual.

In theory, at least, each homeland was supposed to achieve self-government and then independence from South Africa. According to apartheid's advocates, the partitioning of the country allows the various Black nationality groups and races (all of which are now referred to officially as groups rather than races) to live peacefully side by side as independent nations.

The fact is, however, that nearly half of all Black Africans do not live in their designated homelands. And many do not identify exclusively with their nationality group. Many have never lived in "their" homelands. Others are of "mixed" or uncertain nationality. Whatever their reasons, many South African Blacks have no desire to be citizens of poverty-stricken homelands whose governments are perceived to be corrupt, inefficient, and in league with Pretoria.

For those Blacks outside the homelands, the Group Areas Act of 1950 allocates the residential land in so-called white South Africa exclusively for the use of each racial group. Every town and city is surrounded by Coloured, Indian, and Black African group areas. By law, no one may reside outside his or her group area, although in practice many cities have racially "gray" areas because of inadequate housing for various Black groups. By 1991, the government had introduced legislation to

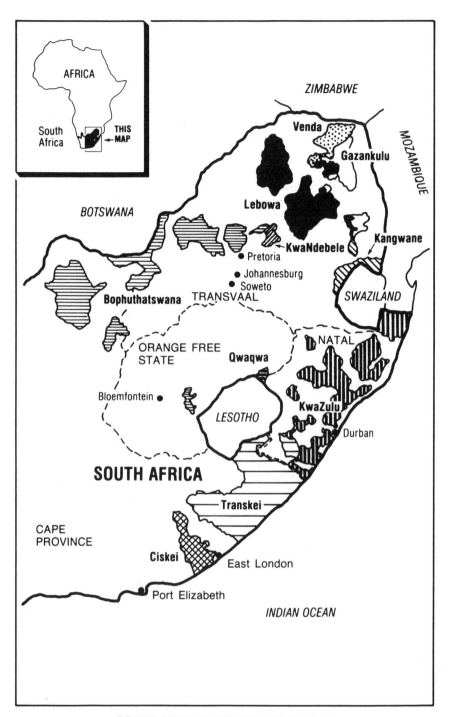

SOUTH AFRICA'S ETHNIC HOMELANDS

Adapted by permission from James DeFronzo, *Revolutions and Revolutionary Movements*
(Boulder, Colo.: Westview Press, 1991).

repeal the Land Acts of 1913 and 1936 (on the basis of which the country is divided into white and Black reserved lands) and the **Group Areas Act**. The territorial or spatial arrangements of apartheid are slated to be demolished.

Accompanying these spatial dictates is an elaborate set of security laws and regulations that mandate and enforce racial separation in social and economic matters. Although much of this scheme, called "petty apartheid," is being reformed and even dismantled, it is hard to visualize significant reform without the repeal of the totality of separate development (homelands), the Group Areas Act, and the Population Registration Act of 1950. The last classifies all citizens into the racial groups on which these dictates rest.

Yet these laws do not show, in terms of flesh and blood, the pain, frustration, and terrible injustices for which apartheid stands. They merely describe the structure of a system that touches virtually every aspect of South African life, whether in the dominant white realm or the oppressed Black "nations."

It is important to realize that the colonists who settled South Africa, and the various colonial regimes in Europe that were charged with maintaining their hegemony in South Africa, had long preferred a racially stratified order based on economic exploitation, social denigration, and segregation of the Black peoples they encountered. Seeking the maintenance of social distance among the races, and yet using the more numerous indigenous peoples for economic and military purposes, was a paradoxical process indeed. What evolved was a complex system of coercion, ideological controls, and economic stratification and exploitation. For the first two centuries and well into the third, it was a relatively ad hoc, hit-or-miss approach to domination. But in this century, after the establishment of the Union of South Africa in 1910—especially when an **Afrikaner** nationalist movement (descended from Dutch and French Huguenot settlers) began to coalesce politically after World War I—the evolving economic structures in South Africa needed a dependable, permanent work force. The booming extractive industries and the rapidly developing industrial sector suffered from the casual approach to racial control and the logic of the British penchant for paternalistic "democracy." An insecure white population had to attend more systematically to the estblishment of certain instruments of political and economic control. The threat of a militant Black proletariat was played up by NP politicians and contributed to the NP's election victory in 1948. Since then the NP has ruled South Africa without significant challenge from its all-white constituency—without challenge until very recently, that is.

The race policies of the Nationalist Party (composed mostly of Afrikaners) were the logical result of the "moderate," preapartheid policies of the white ruling establishment. The term *apartheid* was first coined in 1929. It was used as an election slogan in 1948 and, for a short while afterward, was the official name for the government's race policy. Among its early intellectual apologists at the universities of Stellenbosch and Potchefstroom, as well as at the South African Bureau of Racial Affairs, the argument might have sounded like this:

South Africa is the only homeland for Afrikaners (and for all true white South Africans). We have no desire to move away. Why should we? We have been in South Africa in most cases as long as the Black peoples. We have a right to this land, and we want to preserve our "white Christian civilization" and to maintain our racial identity. But because we are in Africa and surrounded by overwhelming numbers of Blacks, we are threatened with being swamped, culturally and genetically. Integration is out of the question, because it leads inevitably to Black domination and miscegenation. So is majoritarian one-person/one-vote democracy, for that would lead to a Black government and to policies designed to undermine white economic and political power. The only possible salvation is apartheid. The races must be physically separated. Native cultures must be preserved. Blacks must not be encouraged to become "Black Europeans." Establish Black homelands and prepare them for independent statehood. Because the modern economy cannot function without Black labor, however, a Black work force must be accommodated on the fringes of white-controlled cities and towns. Ideally, the Black workers will eventually become citizens of their respective homelands and may return to those "national states" where they can exercise their full political rights and aspirations. Meanwhile, they will be cared for and marshaled by the state and private businesses. If they obey and are subservient, a paternalistic and benevolent white society will treat them fairly. Of course, the white power structure must determine what is fair.

THE WORLD AND SOUTH AFRICA
HEAD IN OPPOSITE DIRECTIONS

The apartheid system was formally introduced in 1948, but it was not until the prime ministership of H. F. Verwoerd (1958–1966) that the state began to pursue these segregationist aims rigorously. "Ad hocery" took a back seat to control and to hierarchical repression. Even Verwoerd himself stated without apology in 1963: "We want to make South Africa White. . . . Keeping it White can only mean one thing, namely White domination, not leadership, not guidance, but control, supremacy."[3] In reality, apartheid means domination, white supremacy, Black exploitation, and political and social repression. In matters of power, status, and wealth, the accident of birth is everything.

Part of what made South African policies a global issue was that the country was swimming against the current of universal values. Moreover, Blacks were not prepared to accept the dictates of apartheid without opposition. Mounting Black resistance highlighted the inhumanities of apartheid. At the very time when the South African government was beginning to systematize and rationalize the racial basis of its power, the majority of people in South Africa and the rest of the world were declaring racism evil. Just when South Africa was entrenching minority rule and making the principles of majoritarianism unattainable and unacceptable, European liberalism was being transplanted throughout the world. The commitment to popular majoritarian government had become universalized. White domination was philosophically obsolete and indefensible in an age of self-determination and adherence to the tenets of color-blind political expression. Truculent minority rule made a mockery of the internationally enlightened endorsement for one-person/one-vote and one-state/one-vote representation in international organizations and meetings. Superficially, at least, South Africa's problem has been one of timing: The principles of governance espoused by Pretoria clashed frontally with those then gaining popularity elsewhere in the world.

South Africa was out of step with changing world values in another respect as well. It was trying to put into place a system of colonies—domestic colonies—in an age of decolonization. Europe's great colonial empires were being dismantled. While vast stretches of Africa, Asia, the Caribbean, and the Middle East were gaining their independence or being prepared for self-government, Pretoria was constructing an elaborate rationale for a system of native reserves that were being turned into homelands, thus effectively creating an internal South African colonial order.

At the same time, South Africa's leaders sought to expand their range of policy independence by severing their links with Great Britain and the British Commonwealth, which was rapidly coming to be dominated by the non-European ex-colonies (not the dominions). Many Commonwealth members wanted to judge South Africa's racial policies and wanted to use their common membership to pressure Pretoria to change. By establishing a republic outside the Commonwealth, South Africa felt better able to fashion a colonial system of its own. Antiimperialism and procolonialism coexisted in Pretoria—under one government.

Other important considerations mark the elaborate justifications for the homeland policy. In addition to the NP's desire to separate Black and white South Africans physically and to rationalize the unequal distribution of land and resources between the races, apartheid thinkers appreciated the emerging appeal of African nationalism and realized that they had to create an outlet for its expression. So they propounded the idea of separate development in order to steer legitimate political aspirations toward divided, weak, and hence controllable homelands that would pose no danger to white minority rule. The proposed pseudo-independence for each dependent nationality group was somehow meant to satisfy the African demands for political rights. The regime sought to endow these rights with a cachet of independence that would defuse world demands for majority rule in South Africa and yet allow fulfillment of the manpower needs of white South Africa. It also brought in vulnerable Blacks as migrant workers in South Africa at the behest of white employers. Not for a minute did Pretoria think that the homelands could survive without security aid and financial and technical assistance. Pretoria wanted to regard the former High Commission Territories, those British colonies in southern Africa administered by the British High Commissioner (ambassador) in Pretoria (Bechuanaland, Basutoland, and Swaziland), as quasi-satellites of South Africa. The homelands would likewise be cultivated as dependent "independent" states. They were to be a safety-valve, offsetting demands for Black power and majority rule by granting a meaningless independence.

Although Pretoria has not been able to sell this idea to the rest of the world, and although most Black South Africans see the homelands for what they are (i.e., sham states), four homelands have already been set adrift. Thus they have had an impact on the way that *some* Blacks think about their political future. Governmental structures have been established in the homelands. Bureaucracies are operating, and entrenched interests, until a recent spate of coups, exercised dictatorial power internally. These interests may not be easy to displace. Indeed, the four "independent" homelands (national states in the official South African lexicon) and the so-called self-governing but not yet independent Kwazulu regime led by Chief Mangosuthu Buthelezi and his well-organized party known as **Inkatha** pose a significant threat to transition to majority rule for the advocates of a unitary South African state. Inkatha is the political party organized by Chief Buthelezi to control Kwazulu and to mobilize the Zulu people both throughout the Natal province and, less successfully, the country.

The rest of the world rightly criticizes these client states and their dependent, collaborative puppet governments. But the longer they exist (the Transkei got its "independence" in 1976, Bophuthatswana in 1977, Venda in 1979, and the Ciskei in 1981), the more difficult it will be to reintegrate their peoples and territories into a single South African state. These governments were originally composed of traditional chiefs and headmen on the South African payroll. They operated under the long-standing imperial principle of "indirect rule," by which indigenous leaders were permitted to occupy positions of authority provided that they worked within the confines established by the metropole. South Africa's response to the coups in the Transkei in 1987, the attempted coup in Bophuthatswana in early 1988, the 1990 coups in the Ciskei and Venda, and the continuing violence in the Ciskei, Bophuthatswana, and Venda give hints as to the boundaries of action acceptable to Pretoria.

When General Bantu Holomisa of the Transkei seized power in a bloodless coup, he merely informed the South African foreign minister by letter that the Transkei intended to respect the Transkei's agreements with Pretoria. He then asked South Africa not to intervene. The South African government recognized the new military government. By contrast, the coup in Bophuthatswana in February 1988 collapsed within hours when the South African Defense Force (SADF) intervened to restore the president, Lucas M. Mangope. At the request of a new military government, the SADF was also ordered into the Ciskei in March 1990 to restore order and to protect government installations. Pretoria refused ex-President Lennox L. Sebe's request to restore him to power. (Sebe was in Hong Kong at the time.) In April 1990, the Venda Defense Force also ousted an unpopular president. The South African government did not interfere.

Depending on the degree of stability prevailing in a given homeland, the popularity of its government, and the degree to which Pretoria feels that it can work with the coup makers, South Africa has been prepared either to do nothing, to intervene to put down the coup, or to assist the coup leaders in maintaining order. Even in cases where the new military governments have expressed support for the revolutionary parties in South Africa and called for the reintegration of their territories into South Africa, Pretoria has not always taken steps to undermine them.

The South African government both implicitly and explicitly understands that the homeland system has failed. It has accepted the fact that independence is no longer an option for the remaining homeland territories not yet "independent." Given the presence of governments in the Transkei, the Ciskei, and Venda prepared to reintegrate their lands into a new South African system, the homeland problem might just be resolved smoothly.

Because societies are dynamic, the philosophies used for social control must continually be modernized to accommodate the changes they undergo.[4] Thus apartheid today is not the apartheid of the founding fathers of the NP. The rigid application of a blueprint for separation according to ideal mandates no longer exists, (if, indeed, it ever did). Although the Conservative Party (founded in 1982) operates as if a purist version of separate development were a live option, a majority of South African whites regard the party leaders as reactionary dreamers at best. The future choices, as seen by most whites, are these: (1) reform of apartheid (and there is heated debate on the nature, extent, and pace of various reform proposals), entailing the dismantling of some apartheid practices and institutions; (2) the replacement of apartheid with an altogether different form of interactive race relations; or (3) the total abandonment of minority control and the search for a nonracial domestic order, as embodied in a multiplicity of proposals and constitutional schemes.

Thinking whites maintain that to do nothing poses the greatest risk of all. In the words of President F. W. de Klerk, "There is no alternative for South Africa but the road of reconciliation and of creating opportunities for all people of this country in a way which is just, fair and equitable. [For whites] to cling to power means accepting the risk—more than a risk—facing a revolution. Nowhere in the world has a minority clung to power without that result."[5] To be sure, South African government leaders have been mouthing platitudes about change and reform for many years. They insist that apartheid is being phased out. Indeed, some have declared apartheid and white domination dead. They still prefer separation, but somehow without discrimination or domination. Blacks, however, want to see deeds, not promises; significant changes, not gestures. The questions relating to segregation are not exactly questions of power; and until the latter are addressed, efforts at reform seem designed to delay the inevitable, not to confront it.

THE STRUCTURES OF BLACK RESISTANCE

Blacks have not been willing and uncritical subjects of white initiatives to entrench white privilege, repressive controls, and racial segregation and exploitation. Just as earlier Blacks fought the original settler incursions into their lands, so twentieth-century Blacks have organized to resist and change the inequitable apartheid order.

Beginning with the creation of the **African National Congress** (ANC) in 1912 and the establishment of Black trade unions later in the 1920s, and followed by diverse contemporary political groupings since the 1950s, Blacks have been determined to avoid becoming mere objects of domination and control by white authorities. Their opposition to apartheid has been active, purposeful and sometimes effective. To these forces we shall now turn our attention.[6]

The Charterist Tendency

The first modern nontribal expression of Black discontent was voiced in January 1912 with the formation of the South African Native National

Congress, which assumed the name African National Congress in 1923. It was an organization of middle-class Blacks (professionals, chieftains, teachers, clerks, labor agents, and so forth) who preferred to try to cooperate with government and to work by means of correspondence, petition, and delegation. They experimented with confrontation only reluctantly, supporting striking workers and collaborating with antipass protesters. After a brief fling with militancy and mass organization in the 1920s, the ANC shifted to a more accommodationist position.

Other militant bodies set up in the 1920s included the Industrial and Commercial Workers Union (ICU), founded in 1919, and the South African Communist Party (SACP), launched in 1921 and based on the Stalinist model. Neither was particularly large, but both had explicitly socialist goals. The ANC, the ICU, and the SACP virtually died out in the 1930s.

World War II and South Africa's industrial boom breathed new life into Black politics. It provided issues around which Blacks could organize. It stimulated urbanization and labor organization. And it contributed to the rise of the National Party and the apartheid state, thereby galvanizing Black opposition to white dominance.

The two most important developments in Black politics during the 1940s were the emergence of the Congress Youth League (CYL) and the consolidation of its influence on the ANC, on the one hand, and the evolving relationship between the ANC and the SACP, on the other. The militant members of the CYL (which was formally established in 1944) were critical of the ANC. They wanted to infuse the liberation movement with "the spirit of African nationalism." The CYL placed its emphasis on indigenous leadership and national self-determination. It was wary of the left and of the communists, partly because many communist leaders were white and partly because the CYL regarded communism as an alien philosophy. Instead, the CYL became identified as an "Africanist" movement, authentic and closer to the masses. Its emphasis on confrontation accorded well with the political climate of the decade. By 1949, its leaders—Nelson Mandela, Oliver Tambo, and Walter Sisulu—had gained important positions on the ANC national executive committee. Communists were still represented on the executive, as were traditional liberal African leaders. The SACP's influence was at its nadir, however. Membership had sunk to 280 people and, as a result of the lack of interest shown by the SACP leadership in Black political affairs in the 1930s and 1940s, African members of the SACP had begun to work within the ranks of the ANC. They pressed the SACP to pay attention to Black issues. Henceforth, the SACP would be identified with the ANC, which in turn sheltered the SACP and appreciated its commitment to nonracialism.

The first mass protests were launched in 1952, and the ANC's membership grew to more than 100,000 people. But as the ANC gained momentum, the NP government began to clamp down on Black activism. The ANC became riddled with police informers, and the Congress had difficulty organizing and managing its activities. Nonviolent mass action was met by repression and violence. Arrests and bannings sapped the leadership.

In June 1955, the ANC and a variety of similar Congress organizations involving other progressive movements (including Indians, Coloureds, whites, and trade unionists) met outside Johannesburg and adopted the **Freedom Charter.** It was later endorsed by the ANC's executive as the party's platform. "We the people of South Africa," the Charter began, "declare . . . that South Africa belongs to all who live in it, black and white, and that no government can justly claim authority unless it is based on the will of the people": nonracialism, not Black nationalism; liberal democracy, not democratic centralism; socialism in concert with capitalism and a market-based economy (there is a nationalization plank on mineral wealth, banks, and industrial monopolies). By this time the Suppression of Communism Act of 1950 had driven the SACP underground. It had decided to affiliate with the South African Congress of Trade Unions and the ANC.

The Africanist Tendency

The **Pan Africanist Congress** (PAC) was officially launched in April 1959. It became the institutional expression of what had been an ideological faction within the ANC. The Africanists opposed what were later called the **Charterists** (for the Freedom Charter), those who favored nonracialism and cooperation across racial lines. The Africanists were determined to motivate the Blacks of South Africa and to free them psychologically from a mindset that was dependent on white leadership. They sought to capture the ANC in 1957 and 1958, and were eventually excluded from the ANC conference in 1958. They then seceded.

Ideologically popular but organizationally weak, the PAC launched its 1960 antipass protests. Its leadership made rash decisions. An ill-planned campaign detonated a political explosion at **Sharpeville** on the Witwatersrand, where the police killed more than seventy people. Sharpeville led to the banning of the PAC and the ANC. The Congress movements were stunned. The PAC was all but crushed. Its ideological tendencies, which were still popular, later manifested themselves in the **Black Consciousness Movement** led by Steven Biko in the 1970s. As usual, the authorities met Black opposition with violence. Biko was murdered in 1977 while in police custody.

Both the PAC and the ANC were forced underground and then into exile. Each independently launched a sabotage campaign that achieved little except confirmation and rationalization of the white government's determination to use force to repress Black political expression. The sabotage campaigns also led to the arrest and imprisonment of their key leaders, including Nelson Mandela.

Throughout the 1960s, Black resistance was largely suppressed. In the 1970s, however, Black resistance was renewed by the rise of political militancy among Black students. From the start, the Black Consciousness Movement involved Indians and Coloureds as well as Black Africans. It found its organizational voice in the South African Students' Organization (SASO), formed in 1969, and in other locally based groups. The SASO joined with religious and educational bodies in 1972 to form a Black People's Convention. Despite its inherently popular appeal, however, it never became a mass-based organization. But the basic set of Black Consciousness catch phrases filtered down to a following broader than that of just intellectuals and students.

An economic recession in South Africa in the mid-1970s led to a sudden rise in inflation, a contraction of the job market, and an increase in labor unrest. Discontent erupted violently in June 1976, when school children in **Soweto,** the gigantic township outside of Johannesburg, protested arithmetic and social science instruction in Afrikaans, which they regarded as the language of the oppressors. The Soweto uprising, as it came to be called, spread throughout South Africa and lasted more than a month. At least 600 were killed and 2,400 were wounded, according to official estimates. The actual figures are considerably higher.

The Nonracialist Resistance

The degree to which the students identified with the ideas of Black Consciousness is debatable, but the uprising and its attendant clampdown forced many young militants into exile. Many joined the ANC and provided that organization with renewed purpose. The ANC reemerged as the political group with by far the greatest measure of popular support in the townships. Many young people underwent military training. In the early 1980s, a series of sabotage strikes was launched, at times against prominent targets. Armed propaganda became the strategy for mobilizing and politicizing the masses.

The next concentrated spate of Black political activity began in 1983. In response to the government's referendum on a proposed new constitution that included a tricameral legislature (one house each for whites, Indians, and Coloureds, but none for Blacks) the resistance movement sought to force a boycott of the election. Opposition spurred the formation of the **United Democratic Front** in August 1983. The UDF was a collection of about 600 organizations that cut across racial and functional lines. Trade unions, civic associations, churches, women, students, and sports groups joined the UDF and, together, pressured government and citizens to dismantle apartheid. They also successfully opposed the August 1984 elections to the Coloured and Indian chambers of parliament—specifically, by preventing voter turnout from reaching expected levels. Community protest on other local issues usually involved UDF-affiliated bodies. The ANC from abroad, with its diplomatic and informational campaigns and its efforts to infiltrate South Africa and the UDF organizing progressive resistance from within, virtually compelled the authorities to occupy the townships militarily. In addition, "comrades" of diverse political commitment and other young militants sought to make the townships "ungovernable." Many townships became armed camps. In others, the police and the SADF could not safely patrol and were totally discredited. Decrees of a State of Emergency eventually covered all of South Africa.

Although the regime was able to enforce a modicum of order on the Black townships by 1987, it was an uneasy and costly calm. Organized Black opposition had driven the NP leadership to acknowledge the necessity and inevitability of change for South Africa, thereby compelling the government to take steps in preparation for genuine negotiations with the authentic representatives of the people.

Yet not all Black political activity takes place within this Charterist, nonracial mainstream. The PAC recovered after it was unbanned in 1990 and, indeed, had never been totally inactive. But it now takes far more uncompromising positions than the ANC. Until the "five pillars of apartheid" (the two Land Acts, the Group Areas Act, the Population Registration Act, and Bantu education) are scrapped, the revived PAC maintains that there can be no basis for negotiation with the government. Despite the militant slogan, "one settler/one bullet," popular among younger PAC supporters, their leadership is less provocative. Many in the movement, however, are hardline socialists who resist any compromise with the current minority regime.

The Subnationalist Tendency

Government's long-standing efforts to divide the Black majority have been and still are partly successful. Traditional leaders, many of whom hold official positions in the governmental/administrative machinery of the state, still exercise some power. They are often in positions of importance, regulating the allocation of houses and building sites, collecting taxes and service fees, commanding council police forces and private vigilantes, and deciding who gets licenses to trade or who gets government jobs. So township councillors do exercise the muscle of local political bosses. But because of their direct identification with the white establishment, their ultimate political influence is bounded. They have no hope of maintaining their power in the "new South Africa." Indeed, most will become vulnerable when popular rule is established.

Far more threatening are various traditionally based politicians who have sought to develop their partisan and territorial base. Chief Mangosuthu Gatsha Buthelezi, the chief minister of Kwazulu (the Zulu homeland), and Inkatha, his cultural organization now restructured as a political party, are the most powerful.[7] As a public official in a homeland, Buthelezi is paid by the South African government. But he has also refused the sham "independence" pressed upon him by Pretoria. He has sought to use his position as the dominant leader of the Zulu people to consolidate his political role in South Africa and to build a large and occasionally violent following.

As the ANC grew in popularity, especially after it had been unbanned in February 1990, it attempted to organize in Kwazulu. Inkatha, in return, lashed out against non-Inkatha elements who threatened their exclusive control of their home turf. The result has been a veritable civil war in Natal/Kwazulu. Since 1987, some 5,000 people (mostly Zulus) have died in the wars there. Then, after August 1990, the struggle broadened to include townships around Johannesburg, prompting the government to reinstitute the state of emergency in that region. Supporters of Inkatha are fearful that they will lose their long-held local status if the ANC, with its goal of a unitary South Africa in which tribal/ethnic identity is transcended, comes to be regarded as the only legitimate representative of Black interests. Inkatha has been able to enlist the support of some Zulus and men from single-sex hostels in the larger townships.

As South Africa approaches negotiations on the future constitutional order, the members of Inkatha have expressed concern that the party may be denied a place at the bargaining table or that its voice may be discounted in the rush to legitimize Mandela and the ANC. But its support is slipping, even in Natal. Its political views and those of Buthelezi have become marginalized, even in the eyes of those who once championed Buthelezi, including F. W. de Klerk, the NP, and the white business community. Still, Inkatha seeks to renew its membership and power. Much violence has resulted from attempts by the party faithful to frighten ANC supporters and to force them to stop organizing in locations claimed by Inkatha. There is evidence to suggest that certain elements of the police have encouraged and even abetted Inkatha members in order to weaken the ANC.

Although Inkatha's people have no expressed commitment to apartheid, their opposition to it is suspect. They operate from a homeland base. They resisted the ANC's call to arms against the regime before the armed struggle was laid down. They insist on playing up ethnic differences. They employ violence and intimidation against those who refuse to join or cooperate with them. And they call for a loose confederal system rather than a unitary one. The ANC feels that this last factor strengthens the advocates of partition and fragmentation. Meanwhile, surveys indicate that Inkatha's following is quite small and geographically bound.

In sum, the Black political struggle today takes three distinct forms, none of which is totally united. First, there is the Charterist group, which is led by the ANC and includes the SACP, the former UDF supporters, and the militant trade unionists. Second, there is the Africanist group, whose weaker organizational expression is identified with the PAC and various Black Consciousness groups, including the Azanian People's Organization. Finally, there are diverse subnationalist groups, which (like Inkatha) are largely ethnically based and many of whose traditional leaders and politicians are entrenched in official governmental positions in South Africa and in the homelands. Each of these groups is divided along the lines of ideology, personality, and economic interest. Most of the groups' members oppose the white government and the philosophy of apartheid. They differ, however, on strategy, tactics, leadership, and ultimate ends. Determination of who, precisely, speaks for South Africa's Blacks is no simple task. Although the ANC-affiliated groups are clearly recognized as the most popular, the other groups cannot be forced to obey or to cooperate; for their followings are in some cases significant, especially in terms of particular regions or among specific classes or ethnic groups.

THE POWER ELITE BEGINS TO CHANGE

It is clear that the neat categorical schemes devised by H. F. Verwoerd and the architects of apartheid are no longer seen to be viable among the NP elite, although some right-wing Afrikaners still work for a return to that outdated order. Most white leaders don't know exactly what to replace apartheid with; and although many have firm and definite opinions, the enlightened among them realize that apartheid has failed them. Past public-opinion surveys have repeatedly shown that the white public tended to be more liberal than the government and the NP on issues of racial integration (of cinemas, schools, sport, and public amenities), on negotiating with diverse Black groups and leaders, and on sharing power with Blacks. As these polls lack specific content, however, it is hard to discern where whites stand on diverse, ill-defined reformist proposals. Opinion seems to shift from month to month as the configurations of power and popularity are altered. The various actors say that they know what they want. But they are not sure what is feasible and do not know how to achieve their ends. In addition, the divisions among all of the racial and ethnic communities are deep enough that every other group tends to reason that it had better not commit too firmly to an elusive short-term aim. The leaders of these groups fear that their followers will abandon or reject them, or replace them with other more current and popular leaders. In this mercurial setting, the process becomes the prize. Black leaders insist on consulting with their people rather than taking the risk of getting too far ahead or behind. A more democratic process is being established, and that is progress of a sort. But for Blacks functioning in an oppressive security-conscious state of emergency, open grassroots organization building has been dangerous. Until the African National Congress and other resistance groups were unbanned in 1990, organization had to be secretive, particularly for the SACP. Even the SACP is now experimenting with public activities.

Pretoria favors negotiating a new "dispensation," but it refuses for political/security reasons to establish a totally open and free political process that would enable truly popular Black leaders to come forth and participate without fear. In addition, the presence of violent rightwing parties poses a threat to Black politicians, especially in small communities. Until a free political process is in place, the spirit of peaceful interaction will be hard to realize.

The important point here is that apartheid, as embodied both in the NP's 1948 election manifesto and in subsequent government policy, is bankrupt—and most white South Africans know it. The various racial communities, it seems, are prepared to search for a formula that will bring them together to resolve the unsettled but increasingly open and negotiable political order. In short, the power issue is coming onto the agenda. But the process has not progressed much beyond opening gambits and bargaining postures. Common ground is still elusive.

WHY IS THE WORLD INTERESTED IN SOUTH AFRICA?

In this fluid setting the world watches and waits and, as it has done since 1948, establishes boundaries, expectations, and demands of its own. The questions remain: Why is the world so keen on following the events in South Africa and so quick to judge it? Why do so many Europeans and North Americans, in particular, invest so much emotion in the events of this relatively small country far from the crossroads of world politics?

There are a number of practical explanations for this interest. Consider the economic category, for example. By 1984, at least 350 major U.S. firms had invested, directly and indirectly, in South Africa—a total of some $15 billion in investments. Far more European, particularly British, firms were and are similarly engaged. At annual general meetings of corporations and of public and private institutions with portfolio investments in corporations doing business in and with South Africa, stockholders and members are often asked, after a fashion, to vote on South Africa. Before sanctions were invoked, the United States had been South Africa's largest trading partner, with around $3.3 billion in trade in 1985. European trading partners continue to be central to the South African economy. Indeed, there is a sense that the West can have a profound economic impact on South African affairs.

The trade issue is complemented by the strategic dimension, for much of U.S. trade with South Africa is in strategic minerals. Chromium, platinum, vanadium, manganese, and cobalt, as well as gold and diamonds, are vital to the West's industrial and military production. South Africa supplies between 30 and 80 percent of the United States' imports of these commodities, and from 40 to 90 percent of the total world's exports.

During the petroleum shortages of the 1970s, the South African government encouraged the argument that the route around the Cape of Good Hope needed to be kept open. An energy lifeline from the Persian Gulf seemed to be especially compelling for Western military planners. Fewer people regard the Cape route as vulnerable today, however. If anti-Western interests are intent on closing Europe's access to petroleum, there are far easier and less risky ways of achieving this end than controlling either the Cape or the South African polity.

South Africa is important also because it has been an arena of East-West (i.e., cold war) tensions. Since the mid-1970s, the Soviet Union and its allies have been involved in supporting the governments in Angola and, to a lesser extent, Mozambique. With communist interest in the region, the cold war dimension became a source of particular alarm to Washington, London, and Bonn. There is a psychological argument, as well. With the Soviets and the Cubans poised to exploit Western lapses and weaknesses, every issue has become a test of the United States' determination and credibility. How would others, including U.S. allies and potential allies, perceive the United States if it allowed Soviet "brazenness" to go without answer? This was a question posed more often in the late 1970s and early 1980s than today.

South Africa is in our minds and on our policy agendas because it poses more starkly than other political contexts the moral questions of our age. Apartheid and the marginal "reforms" that seek to salvage white power and privilege are seen as barriers to the fulfillment of the agreed-upon values of Western civilization. For that reason, Pretoria was regarded in the twentieth century as a pariah, an outcast. Regimes that lack legitimacy and credibility by the standards of the international community do tend to generate a disproportionate measure of opprobrium for their breaches of fundamental human rights.

Outsiders deplore apartheid. Race-based repression somehow seems less complicated than ethnic struggles for self-determination; right and wrong are easier to identify in this context. It demands less of us, less than if we had to face head on the demand that we address in our own societies the more compelling and costly issues of economic equity and redistribution. Those outside South Africa disagree regarding what to do about apartheid at the same time they agree that apartheid is wrong. Americans are being asked to choose how best to deal with South Africa, in corporate board rooms, in church congregations, on college campuses, in trade union halls, and in the salons of Congress, the White House, the state house, and city hall. Many believe that on this issue they can make a difference. Apartheid is clearly wrong, and it is vulnerable. So Europeans and Americans become engaged in the issue because they think their involvement will expedite majority rule and they want to help prevent a horrible and tragically bloody transition. Peace and justice, those twin beacons that have proved so elusive in this changing world, motivate outsiders to speak to the evils of apartheid. For these many reasons, South Africa is a hot item in the news, while Sri Lanka, Myanmar, and the Sudan get buried.

The injustices of apartheid demand change. But the shifting power asymmetries of past years have rendered South Africa explosive. As a group of status quo powers, the West would like to defuse the potential explosion. But a hands-on involvement is required, the means of which are hotly debated. For many, the best way to keep the communists out is to shepherd South Africa through a peaceful transition that keeps the capitalist economic order intact as it revolutionizes the political and social order. To many in the resistance in South Africa these dual aims constitute a paradox that for years prevented Western governments from cooperating with apartheid's enemies in exile.

The importance of South Africa is also evidenced by the extensive media coverage devoted to it. South Africa is in part a modern society. Reporters are there in great numbers, and Johannesburg serves as a center for regional media offices whose technical facilities transmit the news fast. Pretoria insists, despite all its efforts to control and inhibit the media, that South Africa is open to foreign scrutiny. For the United States and Great Britain, moreover, few language barriers exist. Opponents of apartheid as well as authorities are becoming increasingly adept at manipulating the media. South Africa, rather than, say, Peru or Thailand, "looks" important. The more open the media are permitted to be (or, paradoxically, the more they are persecuted), the more coverage South Africa will receive.

Hence, because South Africa is so unsettled, because the Soviet Union has been interested in the region and U.S. foreign policy planners have for years been obsessed with the Soviet challenge, because the resources of the region are strategically important, because Western firms have an extensive financial stake in South Africa, because it hosts a sophisticated and large media contingent, we follow events in the region. But these are lifeless explanations. They lack the flesh-and-blood details that stir emotion and commitment. These sorts of practical considerations apply in other countries, and yet Americans are less aware of and less interested in the domestic matters of these countries. There must be more to the issue.

Indeed, the curiosity of Americans about South Africa grows out of the distinctive features that these two societies hold in common. Americans want to know about and influence South Africa's future because its social problems vaguely resemble our own—a fact that intrigues some and frightens others. Most of us make these linkages subconsciously rather than openly. In the process, we perceive South Africa not so much as a mirror image of the United States but as a manifestation of its worst fear, as if its problems foretell what might happen in the U.S. system if we mismanage our own delicate racial mix.

We may be guilty, as well, of oversimplification, of forcing South Africa's dilemmas and issues into a neat progressive-reactionary model. In other words, we insert our political ideologies into the South African drama. The process makes for antagonists and protagonists with which we are familiar, but it also badly distorts reality. Apartheid offends our democratic values, as it should; so we subconsciously assume that all of those fighting apartheid must share our political commitment to the democratic-liberal values embodied in the Bill of Rights when, in fact, some may be radical, socialist, or violently antidemocratic as well as antiapartheid, at least insofar as Americans understand democracy.

To be sure, many of Pretoria's opponents are committed to the sorts of political freedoms that Americans profess to favor. But make no mistake: Many of those opposed to apartheid are on the far left, and many of them are Marxists, socialists, even Leninists, and are certainly hostile to ideologies of tolerance and an open, competitive political process. In their minds, liberal reformers are too close to the capitalist establishment and too soft in seeking to displace apartheid. The U.S. press often compounds this tendency to gloss over differences between South African and U.S. progressives and among diverse South African groups. They want to see South African revolutionary heroes in U.S. political terms.

Both societies are industrialized. South Africa and the United States share concerns about labor/management relations, wealth and land distribution, urbanization, and the social roles of capital. And as both are settler states, there are ethical issues in common regarding the mobilization and exploitation of an indigenous and/or imported underclass by a dominant culture. Both societies claim to be Christian. Apparently the "enlightened" West senses some paternal responsibility for a culture spawned in Western colonialism that carries out inhumane and exploitative policies in the blasphemous name of "Christian civilization." Both societies also claim to function and govern under the rule of law. Pretoria, despite its hand wringing, asks to be judged by Western standards. And when it is so judged, it complains that the West applies a double standard inasmuch as it doesn't seem to hold Third World or communist governments to the same measures of performance.

As South Africa's government and many of South Africa's apologists in the West see it, ours is a selective criticism born of liberal guilt or prejudice against Pretoria and its embattled white minority. Guilt, in turn, motivates a more active role to offset the years of neglect or, worse, collaboration. Reparations of a sort seem appropriate, and they take the form of proposals to actively undermine apartheid. Moreover, both societies claim to be democratic, at least to the extent that each power elite defines democracy. There is, however, a growing admission by top policymakers in Pretoria that South Africa's democracy is less than complete and that the reform process needs to speak to this concern.

But most of all, there is a haunting similarity between the racial orders in the two states, especially between the historical experiences of the two settler societies in terms of their conquests of their hinterlands and the systems of governance and society that evolved.[8] The slaughter of Native Americans, the dispossession of their land, and their relocation to reservations have distressing parallels in South African history, and South African apologists rightly confront Americans with their historical record. Yet there are obvious differences, too. In the United States a white majority dominates a Black minority. And, according to many Americans, democratic majority rule conforms to principles of governance long championed (though not always a reality) in this country and in other Western democracies. This circumstance supposedly legitimizes our regime. In South Africa, however, a white minority dominates a Black majority. Hence majority rule, at least in a single unitary state with universal suffrage, is regarded by the power elite there as threatening. What is more, the techniques used to maintain white dominance violate U.S. models of ethical governance.

Black against white is an emotional issue—especially for Black Americans and Black Europeans who experience racial prejudice firsthand. And South Africa, in short, appears to embody just such a Black-white issue. Moral outrage is seldom absent. As Sydney Kentridge, a great legal defender of the persecuted people in South Africa, put it several years ago: "Attention is focussed on South Africa not because it has quantitatively less freedom, less justice or less democratic government than a hundred other countries one could name. These goods do exist in South Africa but they are strictly rationed on the sole basis of color—not on citizenship, or birth or merit, but color."[9]

CONCLUSION

The distinctive history and character of apartheid have made South Africa a reviled and lonely state in a world that is paying increasing attention to issues of human rights and the principles of democracy. Whereas the post-1945 world subscribes to the principles of racial equality and majority rule (although it may not always practice what it preaches), the government in Pretoria refused for years to join that world—for doing so would assuredly have spelled the end to a regime that favors South Africa's white minority and exploits its Black majority. Instead, Pretoria constructed an elaborate and, at one time, holistic racial order that touched on, indeed controlled, virtually all aspects of public and, in some instances, private life. Racial segregation and subordination still mark life in South Africa, at all levels—spatial, religious, social, economic, political, psychological, military, and ideological. Moreover, Pretoria's ruling elite have been adept at updating their order. Not until after 1988 did they seriously seek to come to terms with the Black majority and with a critical world community.

That world community, especially the West, has a deep economic, financial, historical, and ethnic stake in South Africa. It wants a peaceful resolution of South Africa's profound injustices. The racial dimension, in particular, runs through both U.S. and European history, and adds emotion to our involvement. As we fit South Africa into our own ideological constructs, we find plenty of parallels to reinforce our predilections. South Africa starkly poses the moral questions of the day, for Americans and for the world. So we follow South African affairs attentively, but seldom with an accurate and undistorted picture of the political alignments there. Among the multifaceted aspects of South Africa, we often see in South Africa what we want to see.

TWO

□ □ □

Changing Perceptions
of South Africa
as an International Actor

S outh Africa was not always an outcast. Indeed, there had been a
time when South Africa could boast an admiring following, especially
among the Western democracies and some of the smaller states. Despite
its policies of racial segregation, South Africa was welcome in Western
councils and, at the United Nations (UN), was regarded as a potential
leader in southern Africa and seen as a reliable military and economic
actor to be courted. How it came to be disdained as a target of external
criticism and meddling deserves review. The South African case illustrates
how a regime's actions can offend the international community and, just
as important, how the very standards of acceptable behavior and the
focus of those standards evolve and impinge on world affairs.

For the past two decades, various elements of the world community
have placed diverse sanctions on South Africa, and its government and
delegates have frequently been excluded from meetings and congresses.
Its sporting teams have been banned from most international competitions, and the UN and even South Africa's most prominent trading
partners have considered imposing mandatory, comprehensive **sanctions**
against South Africa. It would appear that a dramatic shift occurred in
Pretoria's standing. In fact, the deterioration in South Africa's position
was gradual, beginning chiefly at the end of World War II.

Even today, despite South Africa's ideological, political, and economic
ostracization in most Western circles, a lively and often bitter debate is
being waged over the morality and utility of isolating South Africa and

of continuing the work of the private firms and institutions based there. Many consider sanctions seriously only because less comprehensive and less punitive measures to persuade the NP government to institute significant political changes seem to have failed. Among South Africa's regional critics, the debate may be closed, but functional relations with South Africa are still unavoidable. These inconsistencies attest to the strength and diversity of South Africa's economy and to the weaknesses of its neighbors. But they should not mask the level of rejection and disgrace that the world holds for apartheid. The process by which that opprobrium mounted and became an item on the global agenda is the focus of this chapter.

POSTWAR SOUTH AFRICA AS AN ACTIVE AND WELCOME PARTICIPANT

South Africa emerged from World War II, as from World War I, a fully participating member of the victorious alliance and a respected member of a new international organization designed to maintain the postwar order. In both instances, it was the personal stature of General and later Field Marshal Jan Christiaan Smuts that contributed to an inflated role for this remote and relatively small state. Smuts had been a member of the imperial cabinet in Great Britain during World War I, and South Africa had been accorded dominion status in the Common- wealth, along with Canada, Australia, and New Zealand. Later Smuts was deeply involved in drafting the UN Charter and may be regarded as one of the UN's founding fathers. He dispensed advice to peoples and politicians abroad and was widely praised for his liberal outlook. Indeed, Smuts often seemed to have a greater following abroad than in South Africa, particularly among his Afrikaner brethren.

After both wars it was the Indian question—that is, South Africa's discriminatory laws and practices toward its Indian minority—that fo- cused attention on its internal racial relations. At the Imperial Conferences of 1921 and 1923, General Smuts was put on the defensive. Though committed to the empire-Commonwealth ideal of greater cooperation among independent former colonies committed to British cultural and political values, Smuts fought against Indian resolutions that called for equal political rights for all imperial citizens. He realized that if he compromised on Indian rights in South Africa, the logic of denying equality and the franchise to Black Africans would crumble. Political and partisan pressures at home compelled Smuts to urge the conference to affirm the right of each dominion to regulate both immigration and citizenship as domestic questions.[1] This champion of British Commonwealth unity was forced to fight for the empire's decentralization and for narrow racialism. It was a line that his more reactionary successors were to take with pleasure nearly forty years later at the Commonwealth conference of 1961.

Even before that 1961 confrontation, the Smuts government was attacked in 1946 at the UN for its treatment of the Indian minority. South Africa was able to weather the attacks of the interwar period, but it eventually discovered that the international context after 1945 had shifted—largely to the disadvantage of Pretoria.

Two crucial changes of mood and perspective emerged from the wartime and immediate postwar experiences. First, the racist policies of the Nazi government, once the full extent of the Holocaust had been discovered, compelled the world community to question racism and discriminatory state policies. As a result, human rights became a central part of the international agenda, leading to adoption by the UN General Assembly of the Universal Declaration of Human Rights in 1948. Both South Africa and the United States were deeply disturbed by the concerns voiced in the Declaration, and temporary ties developed between Pretoria's supporters and U.S. segregationists. But the central government of the United States did not champion segregation, as did Pretoria; nor was it as vulnerable to external criticism.

The second mood change occurred in response to the demise of the European empires. After 1945, the idea and practice of one people openly governing another against its wishes eventually became morally indefensible. The process of decolonization contributed to the emergence of dozens of new, independent states. Significantly, almost all of these were poor countries outside of Europe. Many considered the racial exploitation and division at the domestic level in South Africa and elsewhere to be a global analog to the north-south, rich-poor, white-Black division of the world. If colonialism did violence to self-determination on the international scene, then racial discrimination extended that violence to the local and state levels. For two-thirds of the world's peoples and their governments, racial equality and anticolonialism became a common, if not major, issue in their external relations.

Other significant structural changes also marked the postwar era. In the 1950s and 1960s especially, the mass of poorer and weaker Third World states gained added importance in world affairs. Until the twentieth century, small states tended to be objects of the power machinations of the stronger states of Europe. Seldom were they consulted, even about their own affairs. But World War II had weakened the colonial powers—Great Britain, France, the Netherlands, and Belgium. The postwar order was marked by the rise of two superpowers that had previously been either too weak, too mistrusted, or too reluctant to become intensely engaged in global power relations. Neither had formal overseas empires in the underdeveloped south. Now, however, the United States and the Soviet Union sought not only to be regarded as global powers but also to enhance that status by trying to entice the new states into their ideological camps and spheres of influence. They courted the economically retarded and militarily weak states of Africa and Asia, thereby augmenting Afro-Asian leverage in world affairs. The end of empire, the rise of the Third World, and the emergence of the USSR and the United States as global powers meant that South Africa, with its bald-faced policies of racial discrimination and its quasi-colonial system of homelands established in the 1950s, found itself increasingly alone and unpopular.

The Third World governments were able to turn the UN General Assembly and even the Security Council and Secretariat into instruments for the pursuit of their collective foreign policy goals. Operating as a bloc there and at other international forums, they tried to create a momentum for human rights, decolonization, and redistribution of the world's wealth. In this unfamiliar and hostile environment, South Africa's policymakers were on the defensive. Moreover, growing global economic interdependence and the electronic revolution in the media and in data transmission contributed to a world (or at least a developed world) desire to know what was happening around the globe and to influence those happenings. No longer was it enough to assert blithely to prying outsiders that domestic issues outside their territories were none of their business. By the 1980s, it had become clear that the "closed" societies of Eastern Europe, the Soviet Union, and China could no longer shut out ideas and materials from the West; why, then, should South Africa, inextricably linked with the Western capitalist economy and founded on a racial model unacceptable to the world community, be able to hold the world at bay indefinitely?

If the Smuts government got a taste of external pressure over the Indian question in 1946, the election of a NP government in 1948 amplified the criticism. The full character of apartheid took time to be developed. The 1950s was a time for enacting and implementing apartheid's ideology into law and practice (see Chapter 1). But there is little doubt that the British refusal to allow absorption of the High Commission Territories (now Botswana, Lesotho, and Swaziland) into South Africa, and the exclusion of South Africa from the West's elaborate alliance system against Soviet expansion, despite South Africa's involvement in the U.S.-UN defense of Korea, were early products of the West's rejection of South Africa's domestic racism.

SOUTH AFRICA TRIES TO RESPOND TO CRITICISM

Pretoria was not unaware of the changing times. The government tried to put a more acceptable gloss on apartheid by seeking to justify the *bantustan* policy as a variant of decolonization and national self-determination. That South Africa was prepared to tutor its Black peoples in the arts of self-government and to serve as midwife in the birth of "independent" Black states, in the process diminishing the territorial scope of South Africa, was portrayed as a selfless act of enlightened statesmanship. In reality, however, these policies were pursued against the wishes of popular Black leaders. They were employed to legitimize and finalize the long-standing device of divide and rule by "balkanizing" (i.e., keeping divided) the internal Black opposition to apartheid in a totally inequitable distribution of the assets of the country. Prime Minister Verwoerd may have been influenced by the changing tenor abroad, but not enough to alter his unbending commitment to orthodox apartheid.

Verwoerd and his successors knew that by further integrating South Africa's economy into the Western capitalist economy—in trade, investment, and technology—the Western governments would be less likely to join the growing pressures from the Third World and the socialist bloc.[2] They were betting that, however important political principle might be, profits would win out in the end. Economic engagement has been Pretoria's strategy for more than forty years. Throughout much of this period, South Africa's ruling elite knew that the country's northern reaches were protected by a secure buffer of European-ruled and white-dominated territories up to the Zambezi River and even beyond.

But such a static view of history was not to last. In March 1960, in the township of Sharpeville south of Johannesburg, the South African police crushed a demonstration against the pass laws. More than 70 Black protestors were shot dead; 178 were wounded. In other urban townships, similar confrontations led to violence. The government responded to the rallies, marches, and organized strikes with repressive countermeasures. It declared a state of emergency and banned both the African National Congress and the Pan-African Congress. Militant leaders were arrested, and others who escaped went underground or into exile to form resistance movements and military wings, to politicize the masses, and to mount sabotage campaigns.

Within ten days, the UN Security Council met to consider the situation. The meeting was requested by twenty-nine African and Asian members. South Africa's delegate vigorously defended his government and rejected the contention that events inside South Africa constituted a dangerous situation for peace and security in Africa and thus for the world. Rather, he said, this was strictly a domestic matter that the Security Council would further inflame if it encouraged agitators and additional demonstrations. A relatively mild resolution was adopted. It recognized that the South African situation, if allowed to continue, might endanger international peace and security. It also deplored the South African government's racial policies and called upon Pretoria to take measures to abandon apartheid and racial discrimination.

The apartheid issue had arrived prominently on the world's agenda. South Africa responded by taking steps to strengthen the regime and rejecting the demands of the outside world. In Verwoerd's words, the government had to choose between "international popularity and the destruction of the White nation in South Africa" or going forward with apartheid.[3] Nationalists, he maintained, must defend their racial policies "like walls of granite."[4] Although the critics were not silenced and the Black population refused to admit defeat, the regime's unyielding and ruthless response worked: The opposition was forced abroad or underground. The white minority reasoned that, by "hanging tough," it would cause the critical world to lose interest and the internal resistance to crumble. Or so it seemed.

In retrospect, it is clear that the white minority possessed a false confidence based on repression of the majority and economic recovery from the initial capital flight precipitated by the Sharpeville killings. A hidden opposition does not mean the absence of opposition; and by this time, the resistance had been forced to move from reformist nonviolence to revolutionary armed struggle. But the government appeared to be fully in control. The sabotage campaign of the early 1960s was crushed, and for the remainder of the decade the economy produced growth rates close to those of Germany and Japan.

THE "OUTWARD" POLICY, "DIALOGUE," AND "DÉTENTE"

The declaration of the Republic in 1961 and its subsequent withdrawal of its application for membership in the Commonwealth marked the beginning of South Africa's progressive expulsion and isolation from various international organizations. Yet its economic achievements and the ease with which Pretoria continued its economic ties with the West and its regional neighbors encouraged South Africa to launch an "outward" movement toward the rest of Africa. It was a policy predicated on a sense of confidence that masked a deeper rejection stirring in Africa. Jack Spence calls the period from 1961 to 1974 "the golden years of South African diplomacy," marked by "confidence within and ambition abroad." James Barber and John Barratt more narrowly see 1965 to 1974 as "the years of confidence."[5] Pretoria had essentially dodged a bullet.

These events must be placed in the context of the rising tide of African nationalism. The first rush of African independence seemed so easy. Between 1956 and 1965, no fewer than thirty-one African states had gained independence and taken their places at the United Nations. But after the mid-1960s, the southward thrust stalled at the Zambezi River, until 1974 the symbolic boundary between Black-ruled and white-ruled Africa. Settler Africa posed problems to Black nationalism that were different from and more challenging than those caused by the colonial empires. Nonetheless, many regarded the struggle of Blacks in South Africa as the extension and expression of the same just desires for freedom, self-rule, and an end to the exploitation of majorities by minorities. The martyrs of Sharpeville formed the vanguard that challenged the exclusive structure of South African society. But they were more than that: They were part of the global struggle for dignity, equality, and self-determination for non-European peoples. That is how the Afro-Asian states viewed the South African struggle, and how idealists in the West saw it, too.

The South African regime, as well, came to appreciate these considerations. It felt confident that within South Africa it could control Black nationalism by a variety of devices, techniques, and structures—a combination of intimidation, ideology, political and economic manipulation, reward, and violence. But it also realized the necessity of somehow deflecting or neutralizing the mounting international outcry against apartheid. It thus sought to capitalize on its economic advantages by playing on the dependence of other territories in southern Africa, thereby gaining diplomatic acceptability along with economic leverage. This "outward looking policy," later called the policy of "détente" or "dialogue," was intended to enmesh South Africa's neighbors in a web of functional and economic linkages so constraining that neighbors would perceive sympathy and assistance to liberation movements (principally ZAPU, ZANU, SWAPO, and the ANC) as too costly to contemplate.

The flaw in South Africa's reasoning was crucial, however. Economic power could not so easily be translated into political power. Although a number of regional countries became even more economically dependent on South Africa after they gained independence (between 1964 and 1980), they were determined not to abandon their racial and ideological brothers to the south. Only Malawi, within the region, was prepared to enter into formal diplomatic relations with Pretoria (1967). Moreover, the armed struggles in Angola (1961–1974), Mozambique (1964–1974), Zimbabwe (1966–1980), which was then officially called Rhodesia by its white settler government, and Namibia (1966–1989) in effect negated

Pretoria's efforts to construct a pliant constellation of southern African states. At heart, Pretoria's domestic racial order was the real reason why South Africa was not acceptable to its neighbors.

WASHINGTON ENGAGES PRETORIA

There was an important by-product of the "outward" policy from Pretoria's viewpoint. South Africa tried to parlay its professed willingness to deal with Black-governed states into a measure of acceptance in the West. Although the Black governments knew that apartheid was still in force in South Africa, some Western leaders were less critical. Some seemed prepared to deal more directly with Pretoria because the NP government had demonstrated marginal flexibility on the issue of its "outward" stance. The key to better relations with Europe, in Pretoria's eyes, was its ability to demonstrate its acceptance in Black Africa. After all, the cold war was at that time important to the West. President Richard Nixon's efforts (1969–1974) to designate regional powers in Africa, Asia, and the Middle East to act as Western agents heightened the political appeal of a South Africa. If Moscow was the principal source of assistance to southern African revolutionaries, then Pretoria, despite its embarrassing racial posture, would try to pass itself off as the most reliable defender of order and capitalism in southern Africa. The relationship would have to be circumspect, but the Nixon administration and the government in London were prepared to tolerate Pretoria as a junior partner in the global struggle against communism.[6]

The secret **National Security Study Memorandum 39** (NSSM 39), adopted by the U.S. National Security Council early in 1969, reasoned that "the whites [of southern Africa] are here to stay and the only way that constructive change can come about is through them. There is no hope for the blacks to gain the political rights they seek through violence, which will only lead to chaos and increased opportunities for the communists. We can, by selective relaxation of our stance toward the white regimes, encourage some modification of their current racial and colonial policies."[7] Such a cold war perspective provided the basis for a policy that encouraged South Africa to liberalize its domestic racial policies but did not pressure it to change radically. Except during the four years of the Carter administration (1977–1981), the philosophy of NSSM 39 anchored U.S. policy toward South Africa from 1969 until around 1986.[8] The United States could not openly sell arms to Pretoria, nor could it directly challenge the more stringent positions of the Commonwealth and various Third World organizations. But South Africa's leaders were led to believe that they would not be abandoned entirely to the pressures of militant and putatively "pro-Marxist" Black nationalism.

South Africa, for its part, sought to appear flexible on matters of foreign policy, even as it remained inflexible domestically. Until the military coup in Lisbon in April 1974 and the sudden collapse of the Portuguese government and its withdrawal from Africa in 1975, South Africa was comfortable with its policy of propping up white settler and colonial rule in the region. Pretoria helped Rhodesia resist UN sanctions and arms embargoes. It also provided economic, military, and intelligence assistance to Portugal and Rhodesia. Yet its economic overtures to its Black neighbors led to the belief that it might be able to normalize commercial and financial links and thereby achieve an acceptable *modus vivendi* with these verbally hostile but economically dependent neighbors.

In short, under Nixon and Ford (the guiding hand of Henry Kissinger can also be observed here), U.S. relations with Pretoria were placed in the context of wider global strategic interests. Although the United States would never admit this, Washington subordinated moral concerns and human rights issues to U.S. economic and geostrategic concerns. But largely because the military coup in Lisbon required a greater imagination in their policy in transitional situations, especially on Rhodesia and toward a more active and vocal set of Front Line States, there was some flexibility during the Ford and Carter years.

Carter and his foreign policy team were more inclined to see African nationalism as a compelling and driving force toward change in southern Africa. They downplayed the cold war preoccupation of their predecessors, although such a preoccupation was not alien to their own views. An awkward tension grew up between Washington and Pretoria, especially after South Africa cracked down hard on political opponents during and after the Soweto uprising of 1976. Although the Carter administration was effective in supporting the independence of Zimbabwe in 1980, it had less success securing the implementation of UN Security Council Resolution 435 (1978) regarding Namibia. That resolution declared the South African administration of the territory illegal and provided for the independence of Namibia under a popularly elected government created after a UN-supervised election.

As the Soviet Union and its allies, especially Cuba and East Germany, became more deeply involved in Ethiopia and Angola (1975–1988), and as they increased their support of the South West African People's Organization **(SWAPO)** forces fighting since 1966 against the illegal South African occupation of Namibia, the Western states tended to return to their cold war posture. Rhetoric against apartheid was cheap, but the Carter administration and Margaret Thatcher's Conservative government in Great Britain largely resisted economic sanctions against

South Africa. This situation made for an easier transition to Reagan's "constructive engagement" than many would assume.

What later became known as the Reagan doctrine, which included the provision of aid, including military aid, to anticommunist "freedom fighters," had solid roots in post–World War II foreign policy. These closer ties with Pretoria and with Pretoria's proxies also coincided with partisan leanings in the United States—especially Nixon's and Reagan's "southern strategies" for capturing the White House and their appeals to conservative opponents of affirmative racial policies, socialism, arms reduction, and the use of economic pressures against authoritarian anticommunists. These changes in policy meant a reassertion of strategic aims over the human rights thrust of the early Carter period, which, in turn, rested on Reagan's anticommunist predisposition.

These cold war messages were not lost on the South African government. It knew that the West was not pleased with South Africa's racial policies and with the political repression there, but it also sensed that it would not be abandoned to what Pretoria called the **total onslaught** from the communist bloc. Pretoria learned how to use its own media and those of other countries to paint an ideological face on its opponents in order to offset its own racist policies and violent repression of opposition.

FROM CONFIDENCE TO SELF-DOUBT

Bolstered by such external support, which Pretoria invariably seemed to exaggerate for internal consumption, a confident apartheid government came to power in the early 1980s. The decade was to conclude, however, in a spasm of rapid change and self-doubt.

The ground for these changes had been laid by the shifting regional balance of power from 1974 to 1980. Independence for Mozambique and Angola, as well as the transition to majority rule in Zimbabwe, highlighted South Africa's isolation in the region and its inability to dictate to regional governments. South Africa's repeated military interventions and occupation of Angolan territory (in 1975–1976, 1978–1980, and 1981–1988) failed to topple the Marxist MPLA government there. South Africa's preferred and supported candidates fared badly elsewhere. Once popular Bishop Abel Muzorewa was rejected in the 1980 elections in Zimbabwe, and the Democratic Turnhalle Alliance (sponsored by South Africa) failed to gain wide popular support in Namibia—in each case despite and because of massive assistance from Pretoria. The armed forces of South Africa and its favored government in Windhoek were unable to defeat SWAPO forces operating out of Angola, even though the SADF and its allies invaded Angola often, occupied large stretches of Angolan territory, and destabilized Angola's economy and social fabric. Although South Africa had not won, it had not lost either.

Politically rejected in the region but still militarily fearsome, South Africa appeared to have temporarily contained the nationalist challenge by the early 1980s. The combination of economic carrots and coercive sticks seemed to be working. Feeling relatively secure, the NP called for a referendum in 1983 to approve a set of constitutional changes that were designed to defuse the reformist and revolutionary zeal. President Botha's evolutionary reforms called for the creation of a three-chambered legislature that included separate houses for whites, Coloureds, and Asians. For the first time, the NP was to include nonwhites in parliament. Yet 70 percent of the population, the Black Africans, were not to be represented in the central government. Many both within and outside South Africa asked, was the glass half-empty or half-full? Or were these measures formulated to divide the Black population and thereby thwart the pressures for democratic rule? The Western powers took a "wait-and-see" attitude.

Renamo, a ruthless band of opponents of the Frelimo government of Mozambique, had been growing in military effectiveness and destabilizing that country outside of the key cities. South Africa was the major source of assistance to Renamo. In early 1984, Maputo was driven to negotiate the Nkomati Accord with Pretoria—ostensibly a treaty of "non-aggression and neighbourliness." Pretoria agreed to discontinue its support and sanctuary for Renamo. In return, Mozambique agreed to terminate ANC activities in its territory. Although subsequent evidence demonstrates that Pretoria surreptitiously continued to assist Renamo, the ANC was forced out of Mozambique. The capacity of the ANC to infiltrate South Africa, mount sabotage attacks, and mobilize within South Africa were effectively diminished.

In May 1984, President Botha toured Europe. It was a tour made possible both by the appearance of movement toward a regional resolution and by Pretoria's apparent willingness to move away from a militarist solution. Botha came to believe that his reform program was acceptable to the West and that he had deflected nationalist demands to the satisfaction of South Africa's principal trading partners and diplomatic associates. But his expectations were short-lived. Internally, the superficial calm imposed after the Soweto uprising came to an explosive end. As the domestic picture deteriorated, South Africa's *modus operandi* came unglued as well.

In September 1984, Black urban areas spun out of control in a cycle of violence and repression. The economic recession and retrenchments lowered already-oppressive Black living standards. There were regional variations, but according to one respected survey, between 1980 and

1985 unemployment increased from 30.6 to 37 percent of the economically active population. The consumer price index rose an average of 14.8 percent per year in this period. Actual income for Africans fell, reflecting a marked plunge in disposable incomes.

The obvious exclusion of Black Africans from both the new constitutional order and the referendum that mandated those changes vividly reminded Blacks that they were still objects, not subjects of the regime. It took no genius to link economic deprivation to the denial of political representation in central government. What did require genius was the mustering of a political voice that could mobilize this discontent and evade destruction by the arms of state.

Dissatisfaction and rejection of cooperation with the system spread nationwide, even into heretofore conservative rural areas. The vehicle for this resistance to oppression was the **United Democratic Front** (UDF), an umbrella organization of hundreds of diverse groups, some racially mixed. Among them were trade union, youth, community, women, student, professional, religious, and educational organizations. The protests were varied—rent strikes, boycotts, work stoppages, marches, demonstrations, vigils, church services and funerals, school closings, and stonings, as well as the controversial people's courts and their punishments and murders (especially the "necklacings") of those regarded as collaborators with apartheid. In some communities, the "comrades," as the young supporters of resistance were called, virtually controlled local affairs. In others, pitched battles were fought between the "comrades" and those identified with the status quo, who were often organized into vigilante groups. Controls on the press were tightened. Arrests and harassments of regime opponents increased in number, along with detentions. The townships were at war—both with the authorities and, because of the Black agents of apartheid, among themselves.

Unable to restore order as it had done in 1960 and 1976–1977, the government declared a state of emergency in July 1985. Though lifted briefly in March 1986, it was soon reimposed and was in force until lifted again in October 1990.

The world reacted with anger toward the government. Sanctions again became a topic of policy debate. The value of the South African currency, the rand, fell dramatically (from R1.07 per dollar in June 1983 to R2.29 in January 1985 to R2.68 in November 1985). Private firms sought ways to withdraw investments from South Africa. Bankers imposed embargoes on new loans. Institutions in the West (churches, unions, universities, and businesses, as well as local, state, and national governments) felt pressure to do something to demonstrate their opposition to Pretoria and their solidarity with the masses and resistance in South Africa.

The Botha government seemed to have no long-range plan to reform the system. In such a situation, the "securocrats"—that is, professional specialists in maintaining order (soldiers, police, intelligence specialists, and the bureaucracies attached to them)—had assumed a central role in South African policymaking. Every facet of public policy was gauged in terms of its impact on security. But although the resistance was again eventually forced underground, the regime came to be regarded as politically bankrupt. Black resistance, though internally divided and stifled, had an external following that refused to let Pretoria reestablish the old order. As a police state was costly to maintain, white South Africa was feeling the pinch, too. The regime felt that it could not easily survive unless foreign investments and trade with the West were expanded.

Internal violence led to "creeping" sanctions. The European Community and the U.S. Congress began the process.[9] Yet the NP seemed more fearful of losing the support of its right wing than that of the outside world. As the government regained the streets, it lost its credibility at home and abroad. Pretoria's continued policy of destabilization of nearby states and cross-border raids (the most intensely criticized were the May 1985 raids on Gaberone, Harare, and Lusaka against alleged ANC targets at the time of the Commonwealth's Eminent Persons Group delegation) demonstrated that the authorities were obsessed by security.[10] South Africa under Botha had reached the end of the road. A change of leadership in the NP and in the country was needed, and the 1989 election came none too soon for the Western world.

The face of Pretoria's leadership was changed during the run-up to that election. The Botha government seemed to have reached an impasse—few ideas, little credibility. Botha was forced to step down as NP leader and later, in August 1989, was removed as state president. In both offices he was replaced by F. W. de Klerk, a relatively conservative NP leader, (or so his record indicated) who had gained a reputation for openness and firm courage.

White dominance in South Africa may be down, but it is not out. The white government is on the defensive. It must demonstrate that it has plans for the future. For its white supporters those plans must include a scheme to protect their rights and, for many, their privileges. For the Western world the plans must ensure a peaceful transition to majority rule as they protect private (meaning capitalist) interests. And for the Black opposition the plans must involve at least an orderly sharing of power—but, for most of the opposition, a transfer of power to the majority. In short, the government must somehow be all things to all people. Is that possible?

Even the NP today claims that apartheid is a thing of the past, that racial domination is wrong, and that Blacks will be afforded a role in central government affairs. "The door to a new South Africa is already opened," the new state president said in 1989, "and it is not necessary to batter it down." During the same year, Justice Minister Kobie Coetsee, himself no dove by South African standards, challenged his NP compatriots in words that would never have been uttered by the NP just a few years earlier: "We say we do not believe in domination—let us put this belief into practice. We say we are a democracy—the time has arrived for us to prove that." He went on to assert that democracy demands that all citizens have equal voting rights at all levels; and that since many Blacks do not have the vote, the situation will have to be changed. Moreover (and this is crucial), the definition of *group* may necessitate the abandonment of race as its only referent.[11] For whatever reason, the de Klerk wing of the ruling party has come to appreciate the need for radical change, especially if it can develop a working relationship with the major Black parties.

Yet it would be unwise to underestimate the current state's resilience and adaptability. It is at a crossroads, but its choices are not fixed. For each concession it makes to the Black majority, it risks losing support among its white constituents, many of whom are prepared to take up arms in violent opposition to their impending loss of status and power. Yet a failure to make concessions would reinforce militant Blacks who feel that their leaders are in danger of becoming collaborators of the NP. Neither side, NP or ANC, speaks for all of its purported followers. And other parties demand, sometimes violently, a voice in the process. South Africa is in danger of spinning apart as the pace of social and political reforms quickens. Through it all, the economy may be unable either to sustain the system or to meet the demands being placed on it.

Pretoria's freedom to act is narrowing, to be sure, but the South African state is still a dangerous instrument, both locally and regionally. There is a sense of movement and change. The outside world assumes that a solution can be found; but there are still many bitter and reactionary South Africans, and the character of Black politics and political expression has yet to be determined. Key actors do not agree on either aims or process. Much of the game has yet to be played out.

CONCLUSION

In this chapter we surveyed the history of South Africa's place in world affairs. South Africa evolved from a respected small power that had been afforded a key place in British imperial and Commonwealth affairs and in the larger but still Eurocentric global community of nations, to an outcast, systematically ostracized by states, international organizations, and private groups. The problem is that Europe was losing its sole claim to leadership in the world. Racism was discredited following the ascendance of the Nazi philosophy of racial superiority in Germany and then the defeat of the Third Reich. Colonialism, too, was under siege. As self-determination was to be applied throughout the world, minority rule became indefensible as a basis for state organization. The Third World emerged from that global commitment to self-determination.

It did not take long after World War II for apartheid in South Africa to become a part of the world community's agenda. No matter how Pretoria sought to repackage apartheid (separate development, parallel development, power sharing), no one was buying. The reality of a privileged racial minority controlling an exploited and powerless majority galvanized worldwide support for an end to apartheid. Pressures rose as South Africa dug in its heels.

Despite its role as a world leader, the United States until recently played only a secondary role in pressuring South Africa. Indeed, the United States has long been reluctant to push Pretoria hard. But badgered by the Third World and by pressure groups in the United States and Europe, the Western states slowly and reluctantly took up the anti-apartheid baton. This mounting opposition was not unidirectional. There were spells, under Richard Nixon and Ronald Reagan, during which the United States experienced major lapses. All along, there had been a reticence to identify with Pretoria's most vocal and militant enemies. In fact, a case can be made that U.S. policy has at times been supportive of the white government's efforts to resist change by offering meaningless reforms. The reason is that Washington, London, and other Western capitals have had an East-West or cold war–dominated vision of world affairs. This vision, in turn, has led to the identification of revolutionary opposition to Pretoria with the socialist bloc. By default, Pretoria fell into the capitalist, anticommunist camp protected, up to a point, by the United States.

Pretoria's unwillingness to accommodate the needs and legitimate demands of its majority, along with the growing effectiveness of the opposition forces, has painted South Africa into a corner. The regional balance of power had shifted after the termination of Portugal's role in southern Africa in 1974 and the independence of Zimbabwe in 1980. With the Soviet Union's new thinking on regional issues, the way was made clear for the West to pressure Pretoria to change without necessarily weakening the West's world position. But even more important, the courageous and massive Black resistance within South Africa forced the NP government to adjust policies and change leadership. By 1988, the time had come to explore alternatives to apartheid—for the white minority to try to salvage white privilege and power, and for the Black majority to be able to seize power and respect. By 1990, the virtual collapse of the socialist bloc and the dramatic changes in East-West perspectives exacerbated pressures for a transfer of power in Pretoria. With the communist bloc no longer poised to exploit every shift in South Africa, the time was ripe for pushing for a new regime.

THREE

□ □ □

A Domestic Issue as an
International Concern

omestic and international politics cannot be separated intellectually, morally, or practically. Nonetheless, many legal scholars, politicians, and some political scientists argue that the sovereign state is the major participant in contemporary international politics and the principal subject of international law. They contend that sovereignty provides the state with authority over which no other power may be exercised legally: The state alone may exercise power over its territory and its citizenry. But while this may be juridically so, the sovereign state has seen the steady narrowing of its realm of exclusive sovereign authority since World War II.

INTERFERENCE IN THE DOMESTIC AFFAIRS OF A SOVEREIGN STATE

A crucial question on the matter of South Africa, and one that the international community has debated since the treatment of Indians in South Africa was added to the UN agenda at the First Session of the General Assembly in 1946, is "to what extent does the international community have the political and legal right and the moral obligation to consider an essentially domestic issue relating to one of its members—against the wishes of that member?"

Like most states faced with international criticism of its domestic policies, South Africa, of course, says "not at all." It seeks legal protection in paragraph 7 of Article 2 of the UN Charter, which itself embodies the fundamental tenets of an international order composed of sovereign, independent states. As Article 2 (7) is the heart of South Africa's case at the UN, I quote it in full: "Nothing contained in the present Charter shall authorize the United Nations to intervene in matters which are essentially within the domestic jurisdiction of any state or shall require the Members to submit such matters to settlement under the present Charter; but this principle shall not prejudice the application of Chapter VII."

Chapter VII, in turn, applies to UN Security Council actions with respect to threats to the peace, breaches of the peace, and acts of aggression. In particular, it spells out the procedures by which the Security Council may take measures designed to employ force or actions short of force to maintain peace and deter or end acts of aggression. Therefore, one possible legal justification for consideration by the Security Council (though not by the General Assembly) of race relations in South Africa is that those concerns pose a threat to peace.

The arguments constructed around Articles 55 and 56 are far more frequently invoked by South Africa's detractors. Thus, "with a view to the creation of conditions of stability and well-being," the UN shall promote, inter alia, "universal respect for, and observance of, human rights and fundamental freedoms for all without distinction as to race, sex, language, or religion" (Art. 55, para. c). Consequently, members of the UN have pledged "to take joint and separate action in cooperation with the Organization for the achievement of the purposes set forth in Article 55" (Art. 56). The UN Charter, in its preamble (drafted in part by General Smuts) and human rights provisions, establishes the need for states to promote "fundamental human rights" and "freedoms" within their boundaries. Subsequent international declarations and conventions (e.g., the 1948 Universal Declaration of Human Rights, which was not agreed to by South Africa, and the 1966 International Covenant on Civil and Political Rights, which entered into force in 1976) contain detailed codes of freedoms to which states are expected to conform.

It is true that in contemporary international law, sovereignty reigns supreme. The UN Charter provides ample evidence that its founders sought not only to recognize the nation-state as the fundamental actor in world politics but also to protect its sovereign rights. Yet there is also ample evidence that the Charter's drafters were concerned about human rights. It appears that in the intervening years since 1945, international law has moved away from a preoccupation with procedures and formalities toward a concept of law that includes substantive rights. "The Rule of Law," the International Commission of Jurists declared in 1959, "is a dynamic concept . . . which should be employed not only to safeguard and advance the civil and political rights of the individual in a free society, but also to establish social, economic, educational and cultural conditions under which his legitimate aspirations and dignity may be realized."[1]

South Africa's case has merit based on a strict or narrow interpretation of the Charter and a static rendering of international law. South Africa also likes to refer to the views of the Charter drafters. This focus on the drafters' views has some appeal to states founded upon European conceptions of the law, which tended to see Articles 55 and 56 as a broadly stated set of aspirations, but ones that could not be used to interfere with a state's domestic affairs.[2] In a nutshell, South African delegates argued that the UN, particularly its General Assembly, is not and was never intended to be competent to deal with the treatment of various racial groups within South Africa.

Early on, when the delegates thought that by confronting their accusers they might win votes or sympathy, they argued that South Africa was being singled out for intervention in the domestic affairs of a member-state. In their words, the UN was applying a double standard against South Africa alone.[3] They took this position in two respects. First, they maintained that with regard to Article 55, only paragraph c, which deals with human rights and freedoms, was applied. Paragraphs a and b, which seek to promote "higher standards of living, full employment and conditions of economic and social progress and development" and to address international social, health, and related problems, including cultural and educational cooperation, were ignored. Thus, they contend, their mostly African and Asian accusers should have serious charges leveled against them. On this count, they pointed to India in particular. As India had been having difficulty feeding its massive population, its economic performance looked barely adequate.

Second, with regard to paragraph c, they claimed that the sponsors of resolutions against South Africa are themselves guilty of discriminatory practices. They named the Soviet Union and others as perpetrators of repression and terrorization. Again, India was singled out, because it had undergone a terribly bloody religious contest that led to partition. The same treatment of some Hindu castes and of the "untouchables" hardly marked India as fit to lecture others on human rights.

South Africa's charges of a double standard were never directly discussed at the UN. South Africa was the primary target of UN resolutions because the political and moral climate prevailing in the world centered on racial matters. (Indeed, most legal systems practice selective enforcement of crime. For example, it does little good for an apprehended speeder in the United States to argue that the police should have stopped another driver for speeding or yet another for having faulty tail lights.) But, more to the point, South Africa was singled out because, since the Holocaust, racial discrimination has rightfully been regarded as particularly loathesome, because South Africa insisted on defending its right to discriminate in law, and also because it had a penchant for trumpeting the merits of racial discrimination for all the world to hear. Politically, South Africa has also borne the brunt of Third World and socialist-bloc ire because it was identified with the West. Since the West was the font of colonialism, and since Pretoria's own approach to its homelands was colonial and it defended continued European rule elsewhere in Africa, South Africa became a convenient surrogate by which to embarrass the colonial powers and weaken the historical and cultural legacies of colonialism, capitalism, racial superiority, and Social Darwinism.

THE WEST JOINS WITH THE THIRD WORLD MAJORITY

The Western governments slowly began to change their views and their votes and to join the overwhelming majorities supporting resolutions against South Africa. Their reasons were many, including the desire (1) to demonstrate to the newly independent governments of the Third World their commitment to liberal democracy; (2) to display their growing awareness of the repugnance of apartheid; and (3) to express the belief that external pressure might actually influence Pretoria to reform its racial order. These reasons in turn were based on the realization that open support for Pretoria would be too costly in the goldfish-bowl diplomacy of the UN.

General Assembly resolutions during the UN's first twenty-five years spoke to three major issues involving South Africa: the treatment of Indians, the policy of apartheid, and the South African administration of South West Africa/Namibia. Later, more specific resolutions of censure, condemnation, and appeal touched on subjects such as individual political trials and sentences, release of detainees, weapons sales and tests, embargoes, and trade relations. Still later, specific action-oriented resolutions (e.g., urging members to break diplomatic relations and to cease making available their facilities for South African planes and ships) were passed. In 1979 alone, eighteen General Assembly resolutions against apartheid were passed. The number and specific content varied from year to year, but all were carried by overwhelming majorities—some unanimously. The Security Council also passed more biting and demanding resolutions. In 1963, for example, a resolution calling for a voluntary ban on the sale of arms to South Africa was passed (S.C. Res. 181) with the support of both the United States and the United Kingdom. Its impact, though not total, was significant.

The efforts by members of the **Organization of African Unity** (OAU) to sponsor punitive resolutions against South Africa largely failed until 1977. Not that the members were unable to secure the votes for passage. That was easy. Rather, they came to realize that if the Western powers failed to cooperate with and implement such resolutions, their impact would be marginal. Moreover, vetoes by the permanent members of the Security Council could thwart their designs. To secure votes and, more important, compliance, they found it necessary to negotiate compromise resolutions more moderate and attuned to Western interests.

The murder of Black Consciousness leader Steven Biko by South African police in 1977 and the subsequent security crackdown on dissidents compelled the international community to display a firm and unified disapproval. Still, the Security Council's Western members refused to declare South Africa to be a "threat to the peace," and on October 31, 1977, the United States, the United Kingdom, and France vetoed in the Security Council three Africa-introduced resolutions proposing harsh economic sanctions (including a ban on foreign investments and arms sales, an end to cooperation on nuclear development, and a revocation of licenses to manufacture weapons).

A few days later, however, the Western members joined the Third World against Pretoria. On November 4, the Security Council agreed on a revised resolution that made an arms embargo compulsory on the grounds that Pretoria's acquisition of such weaponry would constitute a "threat to international peace and security." This was the first time that mandatory sanctions had been ordered against a UN member under Articles 39 and 41 of the Charter.[4] In compliance with the ban, France canceled delivery of two submarines and two corvettes ordered earlier by South Africa. The General Assembly then decided, on December 16, to ask the Security Council to impose an oil embargo against South Africa because of its continuing shipments of oil to Rhodesia, in violation of a UN prohibition. A few days later, Canada introduced trade sanctions against South Africa. The South African government began to realize that its ostensible "protectors" in the West were not prepared to stand by the Republic in all circumstances. It was a rude awakening for some who hadn't really understood the changing mood and dynamic process of Western governmental politics.

The Western powers were clearly embarrassed by South Africa, with which they were identified in Third World and socialist-bloc rhetoric. It is true that Western governments criticized apartheid and condemned repressive enforcement measures in South Africa. But these were seen as merely verbal gestures. The West's tendency to finance, trade with, sponsor, or condone personal and technological exchanges, and to resist the isolation of Pretoria, were practical policies on which the rest of the world focused. These were essentially status quo measures that had generally proven profitable to Western institutions and governments. Hence, whenever Pretoria's policies led to unsavory headlines, as in the Biko murder and the subsequent violent repression of dissent, the Western governments felt betrayed and embarrassed by South Africa. They believed they were called upon to demonstrate tangibly their commitment to human rights and political democracy. In other words, they were pushed toward abandoning lucrative (in the short term) but increasingly awkward links with South Africa.

The more conservative elements in Western governments were fitfully being squeezed into a corner. Their predicament sometimes took the form of pressing Pretoria quietly to be more sensitive to outside opinion— to be more accommodating, simply for the sake of public relations. Why, they seemed to ask, must Pretoria "shoot itself in the foot"? Why can't it appear to be flexible and thereby enable the West to deflect the pressures it faces in buffering the criticisms against Pretoria?

UN votes, it must be pointed out, are sometimes viewed as an international version of office politics. A state's declared allegiance does not always or necessarily represent its preference or prejudice. Rather, a vote may be a public declaration that is tempered by private, behind-the-scenes behaviors contrary to its public posture. Some governments, for example, vote for an arms embargo but evade the spirit and/or letter of the law. But this is not always the case with UN votes, nor does such a cynical interpretation reflect all Great Power postures at the General Assembly and the Security Council. Still, Third World leaders have come to see the utility of negotiation and compromise in order to draft resolutions that the West can support both in principle and when votes are cast.

There is, however, a dual and potentially offsetting long-range impact of piling vote upon vote on South African issues. On the one hand, such votes focus the world's gaze on the issue, on conditions in South Africa. Accordingly, outsiders can learn about the realities of apartheid, reason through possible outcomes, and in some cases take actions (often privately) to rectify the injustices. On the other hand, there is the danger that repeated passage of resolution after resolution, especially with little tangible impact on the problem itself, may debase UN deliberations and lead to the cynical conclusion that either the issue isn't really important or that the international community is helpless to rectify the evil at hand.

In the case of South Africa, both results seemed to have occurred. South African leaders became complacent, almost disdainful of UN resolutions and actions. In the process, they chose to ignore the growing atmosphere of rejection and condemnation. In such an atmosphere even

South Africa's business partners, states inclined to protect South Africa or to soften its growing ostracization, found it difficult to be seen relieving the pressure on Pretoria. Indeed, in an era of decolonization, settler minority rule could not openly be defended. The prevailing moral code no longer accepted the governance by one people of another against its will, especially given that those in power came originally from across the sea to seize the land of a more numerous and racially different people.

SOVIET POLICY TOWARD SOUTH AFRICA

If the West is discomfited by its historical and commercial associations with Pretoria, the socialist camp has sought to exploit that chagrin by publicizing and denigrating the West to socialist-camp advantage in the Third World. Socialist-bloc assistance to nationalist/revolutionary parties in South Africa, Namibia, and Zimbabwe, and to the Marxist governments in Angola and Mozambique, coupled with the diplomatic efforts of the socialist-bloc countries to weaken settler governments in the region, served the multiple ends of unsettling southern Africa, ingratiating themselves to actual and aspiring governments, weakening South Africa (and thereby its Western associates), and paving the way for enhanced socialist-bloc involvement in the area. These policies contributed to the Soviet Union's effort to be recognized as a global power, on a par with the United States and deserving of an equal role in affairs of state the world over.

In the hierarchy of world affairs, Moscow ranks Africa fairly low—below Europe, East Asia, and the Middle East—in terms of geopolitical importance. Nonetheless, Africa presents the Soviet Union and its allies with opportunities to expand Soviet influence and to undermine the West and China. Unfortunately for Moscow, the Soviet Union is not now in a position to take full advantage of the opportunities so presented. Soviet policy in the region is generally low risk and low cost. Its overall policy puts the security of the Soviet Union (and, while it existed, that of its contiguous empire) first. Only when these goals had been ensured were resources allocated for enlarging the Soviet role in southern Africa. Although Soviet-bloc presence in Angola and Mozambique had been alarming to foreign policy planners in South Africa and the United States the overall direct Soviet commitment had been limited. At times, the 20,000 to 50,000 Cuban military personnel, the few hundred bloc military advisers and technical assistance personnel, the costs to equip and train a few thousand SWAPO and ANC fighters, and the costs of supporting the ANC, SWAPO, and ZAPU diplomatic and information/propaganda activities provided considerable foreign policy mileage for

Moscow and its allies. What is more, since Angola paid for Cuba's assistance and military materiel in hard currency earned from petroleum exports to the United States, the costs of the military operations to the socialist camp were acceptable. As far as possible, the Soviet and Cuban military personnel tried to avoid any direct confrontation with invading South African forces, thereby reducing the risks of a need to escalate their commitment to their southern African friends.

In many respects it was an ideal arrangement: At almost no cost, the Soviet Union could exercise inordinate influence in a region relatively important to the West. Moreover, by identifying with the Black states against minority colonial and settler regimes and their Western collaborators, and by labeling the West (particularly the United States) as "the bulwark of militarism and reaction" propping up the hated apartheid order, the Soviet bloc reaped benefits throughout the Third World.

Pretoria's repeated charges that South Africa had been subjected to a "total onslaught" orchestrated by Moscow played into Soviet hands, for South Africa gave the socialist bloc undeserved credit for virtually all opposition to apartheid. In so doing, it ensured a Soviet bloc presence in the region; and this, in turn, guaranteed a U.S. preoccupation with the cold war dimensions of the issues.

The cold war distraction reached its apogee during Ronald Reagan's first term, when Assistant Secretary of State for African Affairs Chester Crocker developed the concept of "linkage." It was proposed in the form of an agreement by the United States to get the Cubans out of Angola in return for a South African commitment to implement the UN plan for Namibia's independence. UN Security Council Resolution 435 of September 1978 called for a cease-fire between SWAPO and the SADF and its proxies, for UN-supervised elections, and for Namibia's independence—an arrangement that eventually bore fruit in 1989 and 1990.

At the time, the South Africans were quite taken by the "linkage" formula. It enabled them to deny responsibility for a lack of settlement in the region. It also allowed the SADF and **UNITA** to foray widely throughout Angola, thereby making it difficult for the Angolan government to accept Cuban withdrawal. Thus the South Africans were in a position to ensure a Cuban presence and, hence, to argue that others were to blame for the delays in Namibia's independence. The Cubans were the tangible proof that the "total onslaught" was real.

Throughout the first seven Reagan years, the intrusive powers (Cuba, the United States, the socialist bloc, and South Africa) seemed to be secretly content with the stalemate. The people of Angola and Namibia bore the burden of protracted warfare and economic strangulation. By the end of 1987, the diplomatic impasse was firm. Within the year, however, two interlocking accords had been signed by the military actors directly involved—Cuba, South Africa, and Angola. These accords were brokered in large part by Chester Crocker and seconded by the Soviet Union. A fortuitous combination of strategic, political, military, and economic circumstances contributed to the settlement. Among them was an important shift in Soviet foreign policy under Mikhail Gorbachev that led to an effort to reach accommodation with the United States on a number of long-standing regional disputes. Overall, however, the Soviet Union seemed prepared to scale back its regional commitments in order to concentrate on domestic and East European problems, both economic and political.

CONCLUSION

In the field, a military shift in power relations put South Africa's forces on the defensive. The 1987 Angolan offensive against UNITA and the South African forces in southeastern Angola was bogging down. The siege of an Angolan forward base and strategic airfield at Cuito Cuanavale led Castro to commit experienced troops to front-line combat for the first time. These 15,000 new troops tipped the balance, and all along the front the South Africans were under pressure. Equally important, the South Africans had lost air supremacy, thanks to a sophisticated radar system recently emplaced in southern Angola. South Africa began losing precious aircraft, which were difficult if not impossible to replace in the face of the arms embargo. Pretoria came to realize that the rising costs of the war in Angola and its occupation of Namibia required it to entertain proposals for negotiation.

Almost simultaneously, the various combatants seemed to sense that they were fighting an unwinnable war. In South Africa especially, the war became a controversial and partisan issue. The costs of war, combined with the impact of financial sanctions, were taking their toll. When the superpowers joined in a massive diplomatic effort to reach agreement among the parties, signals were exchanged and in May 1988 formal negotiations among Cuba, Angola, and South Africa were begun. Meetings in London, Cairo, New York, Geneva, and Brazzaville sharpened the issues. A final agreement in December, called the Protocol of Brazzaville, applied to two peace treaties and was signed at the UN. One was a tripartite agreement that provided for Namibia's independence under the UN plan. The other, involving only Angola and Cuba, stipulated the schedule for Cuban troop withdrawal from Angola. The United States and the USSR became guarantors of the treaties. Crocker's persistence paid off, for he originally launched his efforts as far back as April 1981.

These events reinforce the argument that, in diplomacy, timing is crucial. It so happened that each of the central actors was ready to compromise: In the words of William Zartman, southwest Africa in particular was "ripe for resolution."[5] South Africa's willingness to participate in the Angola/Namibia settlement, though largely a coerced willingness, provided Pretoria with breathing space and freed up resources with which to address domestic issues and to rethink its regional and global posture. Again, timing was crucial. All of these events occurred as the NP was undergoing a leadership crisis (in January 1989, President Botha suffered a coronary) and a general election was called for September 1989. In short, a shifting regional context, domestic white partisan confusion, and increasing Black militancy (following a period of particularly coercive repression) combined to enable and require foreign powers to reassess their policies toward South Africa.

FOUR

□ □ □

The Economic Dimension

outh Africa occupies a distinctive place in the capitalist world economy. That functional locale underlies the policies pursued by Western governments toward Pretoria and helps explain the difficulties they have had in framing an effective and unambiguous position on apartheid.[1] The following section utilizes a variant of world systems theory, occasionally called dependency analysis. Though not universally accepted and seldom applied to South Africa, this model does provide insight into South Africa's uneasy relationship with the Western governments and economies.

SOUTH AFRICA IN THE INTERNATIONAL GLOBAL POLITICAL ECONOMY

The Western powers may be regarded as the core of the global capitalist system. Collectively, that core dominates the periphery, which includes virtually all but the socialist states (and even this exception, of late, may be subject to modification). It dominates financially, technologically, militarily (although military power may not readily be applicable), productively, organizationally, and culturally. The rest of the world, for various reasons, adjusts and adapts to the decisions of and structures controlled by the core. In the economic realm, peripheral actors tend to produce raw materials for export and to be penetrated by economic institutions based in or directed from the core. Despite their profound differences with the powerful core, the peripheral states do not always compete with it. Their dependence is often founded upon a symbiotic relationship between the dominant institutions in the West and local elites that control peripheral states. Both dominant elites profit from this relationship, largely because of their ability to exploit the labor and vulnerability of the powerless majorities in these territories.

When it is working smoothly, this arrangement is a sophisticated twentieth-century version of indirect rule, the effective policy of Rome and other empires by which indigenous political structures were enlisted to maintain order on behalf of the metropole. In the contemporary version, formal or juridical bonds are replaced by no less effective structural ties (e.g., direct and indirect investments, financial aid, marketing and distribution arrangements, technical, cultural, and educational exchanges, and so forth).

But not all periphery governments take comfort in the knowledge that their privileged status depends on their ability to exploit their own peoples and on their willingness to be identified with an economic system dominated by the West. Their own elite status is seldom secure. Therefore, they must not only seek for their states a greater share of the unequally distributed wealth of the global economy but also somehow demonstrate that they are nationalists first, prepared at times to challenge the West. Antiimperialist rhetoric, votes at the UN, even expropriation of foreign-owned enterprises (especially natural resources or other symbolic national assets such as canals) serve to distance these governments from the core. In the contemporary era, however, core institutions have proven to be extremely adept at staying several steps ahead of their clients and dependents in the Third World. One tool for accomplishing these ends has been to keep peripheral states divided, each seeking favors or special advantages over other, more vulnerable, actors.

Dependence is a matter of degree. States are more or less involved in the system, depending on the inequities of exchange and the structural stabilities that underlie their behavior. As conditions constantly change, some states may begin to aspire to positions closer to the core. Some periphery governments may perceive that the most effective role they can play in the larger system is to serve as intermediaries between the core and other, still more marginal, periphery states. Such a role would be particularly lucrative if there is room for maneuver in the interstices between individual core systems (e.g., between British and U.S. actors) and between components of the overall system (e.g., between a single corporation and its more remote clients).

Thus a state may simultaneously find itself in a peripheral relationship to a core state or states and in a core-like relationship to other periphery states. Such intermediary relationships actually facilitate the operations of the total system—for instance, by maintaining strategic order in a region or by serving as a regional conduit for raw materials and finished products in a three-cornered exchange. Brazil has played this role as an intermediary for U.S. core activities in Latin America. Other examples include Mexico in Central America and Iran, during the Shah's reign, in the Gulf region. In Asia, Hong Kong and Singapore have served British interests well, as has South Africa in southern Africa in years past.

In some territories, colonial settlers have been a vital intermediary force, especially when they have been able to establish entrenched minority regimes. These groups—including settlers, the administrative machinery of the expatriate mercantile-extractive complex, the local staffs of metropolitan-based companies, the lower levels of the colonial civil service, and the supporters of these interests in the metropolitan state— emerged as "independent" factors that insinuated themselves between the core governments and the indigenous peoples of periphery states.

Although in most cases the colonial settlers came originally from the mother country, there was never a precise coincidence of interests between these elements and the metropolitan government. After the core's leaders decided that direct administration of colonial territories did not add to the advantages derived from a territory relative to the costs involved, they determined to grant independence (usually to selected and reliable elements of the indigenous population). Colonial settlers in some territories then seized the moment to claim independence and thus end the encumbrances posed by empire. (Indeed, a minority regime in an independent state can more openly exploit and control the indigenous majority.) Had independence been granted to the majority, as the imperial government proposed, the colonial settlers would have been the most immediate losers. So they challenged the mother country whenever it appeared that the latter was making policy based on considerations of their wider, global economic and political interests. In short, colonial settlers became antiimperialists within the global context in order to facilitate, prolong, and strengthen their own provincial or domestic "imperial" system. By seceding from the British empire (as in the case of South Africa and, later, Rhodesia), the colonial settlers could be free to repress and exploit more completely the majority in their territories— for them the element posing the greatest threat.

SOUTH AFRICA'S AMBIGUOUS INTERMEDIARY STATUS

South Africa behaved for years as an intermediary state. Its economy, partially industrialized and partially a producer of primary products and raw materials, is ahead of most Third World states on the productive ladder; yet the country is still several steps behind the Western industrial states. South Africa imports unskilled labor from its less-developed neighbors, yet it depends heavily on capital, products, and technology emanating from the core. It exports processed and finished products and, to a lesser degree, investment capital to its neighbors, yet it must sell its raw materials to more advanced economies. In short, it is neither peripheral nor central in the global political economy. For years this circumstance generated an ambiguous combination of foreign and domestic policies, some reflecting a harmony with the Western core and some conflicting with core policies.

There is an additional reason for this intermediary status. South Africa's settlers are diverse. Racial affinities have been complicated by nationality differences, especially between Afrikaners (of Dutch and Huguenot origin) and English-speakers. In response, National Party governments (representing largely Afrikaners in the past) have been prompted to regard Great Britain not as a mother country but as the imperial enemy. However, the powerful British-rooted economic interests did not want to abandon Great Britain or Britain to abandon them. They hoped to enlist the West in the cause of perpetuating their economic advantage. Today, these two elements of white South Africa are coming together. Afrikaners are increasingly entering the commercial/financial realm, and English-speakers are identifying more often as South African nationalists.

In addition, South Africa has sought to become more self-reliant— partly as a function of having been excluded or ostracized by the rest of the world, and partly in an effort to preempt and offset the growing effects of sanctions and disinvestment. Other factors include its calculated policy of autarchic development, the postwar economic decline of Great Britain, and the opportunities presented for a more vibrant economic leadership role in the region. Until recently, other core states (the United States, Japan, Germany, and France) and their institutions were prepared to move in on Britain's domain.

For awhile, Pretoria was able to attract, and to define the terms of, foreign investment and trade. By creating governmental corporations in important economic and military sectors, by investing in infrastructure and directly in foreign-based private firms, by forcing or encouraging foreign capital to accept degrees of local participation, content, and control, and by redefining the terms of trade with the core countries through adjustments in tariff and licensing policies, South Africa was able to gain greater independence from the West as it became drawn more completely into the capitalist global economy.

During this period from 1950 until 1980 or so, there really wasn't much resistance from corporate executives and directors in the core. Indeed, they were content to allow Pretoria to enforce social policies that contributed to the profitability of their investments. They could wring their hands and criticize the evils of apartheid and still cash in on the advantages of a cheap and compliant labor market and accessible raw materials. As long as the South African economy was booming, the West could find ways to rationalize the status quo in the region. But when the goose stopped laying golden eggs, it was time to think about exchanging the goose. This, in effect, is what began to happen in the 1970s and 1980s.

The prolonged world recession, which began after the OPEC petroleum price increases in 1973–1974, had its effects on South Africa. As the advanced capitalist economies contracted, there was less demand for South Africa's raw materials. The prices of raw materials fell at the same time as inflation abroad contributed to higher prices of imported manufactured goods. As trade abroad accounted for a high percentage of total GNP in South Africa, and as it relied heavily on imported oil, the international recession hurt. But it was chiefly the high price of gold throughout this period that offset the worst effects of the recession. Gold accounted for more than one-half the value of all exports in 1980. This fact, and South Africa's solid credit rating, expedited borrowing abroad and shielded many firms as well as the government. Still, the decline in the import of capital equipment needed to expand productive capacity took a long-term toll on the economy—a toll compounded by the more complete economic sanctions that occurred later in the decade.

It is important to realize that each of the various economic policies and pressures devised by foreign interests to move South Africa away from apartheid serve multiple ends, depending on the individuals and the groups involved. For instance, a measure designed to oppose or isolate apartheid may provide the party using it with considerable leverage over South Africa, certain South Africans, and the government. By contributing to the abandonment of particular policies, politicians, or interests in South Africa, it may ultimately undermine the purpose for which it was originally invoked. And if such a measure demonstrates the instigator's willingness to bear costs for principle (a public relations plus), it may serve political and economic interests in the country where it is enacted and beyond. A progressive posture against apartheid opens doors among those who favor such positions. Thus an economic virtue may be made of political necessity.

In the context of domestic South African politics, pressure from abroad may be used either to further isolate South Africa from foreign interests or to enable those otherwise open to change to justify reform. Thus, for example, the **Sullivan Principles** calling for U.S. companies with investments in South Africa to desegregate their work places, among other things, also enable South African reformists (even some in the NP) to institute changes under the guise of being forced to do so by foreign interests. Pressure for change has been read, by some, as a license for change. And external pressure has become a tool used by South African politicians.

DISINVESTMENT

The Link Between Pressures and Falling Profits

The performance of foreign firms in South Africa also declined during this period.[2] The average rate of return on direct investment for U.S. firms in South Africa during the growth years had been steady (between 1960 and 1974, it ranged between 16.3 and 20.6 percent), secure, and low risk. By contrast, rates elsewhere in Africa fluctuated between 3.6 and 45.4 percent.[3] Elsewhere in the world, U.S. investments steadily rendered between 10 and 11.4 percent on capital investment. Beginning in the middle 1970s, however, profit margins in South Africa began to fall. As a result of this circumstance, along with growing civil unrest (especially in 1976–1977 and 1983–1986), labor-management conflict, and unfavorable publicity (in other words, greater risk), the reduced rates of return were deemed by many firms to be insufficient to justify either new investment or extensive reinvestment of profits. Driven by adverse economic performance, these firms had to reconsider what was proving to be politically embarrassing and costly in terms of public relations.

According to the Business Environment Risk Index (BERI), which is compiled annually by F. T. Hamer of the University of Delaware, South Africa in 1973 ranked tenth among forty-two countries in overall safety of foreign investment. By 1981, it had fallen to sixteenth place in the area of business risk factors and to twenty-seventh out of forty-five in the political stability category. The premium for risk—that is, the higher return on investment exacted in situations of greater risk—was not adequate to attract and hold investments. This situation, combined with greater external pressure to disinvest from South Africa (from investors, employees, customers, and public opinion in the home country), had a corrosive effect indeed.

The call for foreign-based corporations to end their associations with and apply pressure to South Africa originated essentially among private groups. It complemented the call for Western governments to take action against apartheid as well as the plea for greater support among groups, firms, and governments for the efforts being made by majoritarian forces within South Africa. In other words, corporations were potentially seen as points of economic leverage against apartheid. The corporate fulcrum was merely one of the most visible and, because of the profits involved, ostensibly one of the most culpable links between the West and the regime in Pretoria.

Even among those who claim to be opposed to apartheid, the arguments regarding corporate involvement range from the goal of maintaining investment and using a firm's presence there for social betterment to a total closure of operations and a severance of all business links—engagement versus isolation. The question is whether foreign investment should be encouraged or discouraged and, in either case, what standards of social responsibility should be upheld by which firms. A number of vocal critics have latched onto this issue. Seeing nothing useful in capitalism, they demand that firms get out in order to prepare the ground for a socialist revolution. But such an argument is offset by the counter-viewpoint that capitalists can do no wrong and, hence, that a capitalist presence is indispensible for any growth. To procapitalists, the market alone should determine how investments should be allocated.

Critics charge that foreign investment reinforces the South African regime, materially by providing much needed capital, technology, trade, and contacts; and psychologically by enabling Pretoria to argue that it still has important associates prepared to cooperate economically and to risk their treasure. Moreover, firms pay taxes to the government and serve as insurance against economic sanctions, and foreign loans help cover purchases abroad. In addition, U.S. investments, especially, have tended to be in such key industries as automobiles, computers, energy, and mining—industries critical to regime maintenance. Especially when outsiders were making huge profits, the price of some verbal abuse from moralists and social gadflies was tolerable. But critics also focus on the long-range impact on Western foreign policy and on individual firms' relations in the Third World, especially in Black Africa. Is there a danger, they ask, that the West might become enmeshed in the defense of apartheid as these governments seek to protect the investments of firms based in their countries? Indeed, continued corporate presence undermines the official rhetoric of antiapartheid.

The potential of racial war and regional unrest has long been close to the surface. When profits soar, the cold economic arguments are on the side of those who wish to stay. To withdraw, to sell out, they contend, would involve taking an unnecessary loss. Moreover, less socially conscious firms from other countries would seize the opportunity, at a discount, to displace their competitors. But, say advocates of disinvestment, you have to be prepared to pay a price to back up your morals with action.

As pressures on these firms mounted, the firms altered their arguments somewhat. They retained their economic concerns, so as to please their shareholders who demanded return on investment. But they also began to introduce arguments designed to appeal to socially conscious observers. Among these were the assertion that Blacks would suffer more than whites if firms were to disinvest, that foreign companies pay better wages and have more enlightened working conditions than do South African firms, that foreign companies are deeply involved in social action programs designed to break down apartheid structures, that they have begun to sever their links with South Africa's governmental agencies (especially the police and defense forces), and that they are working, less publicly, to be a political force to end discrimination, exploitation, and political repression. Thus, they contend that foreign firms, far from being collaborators with apartheid, are positive forces for reform.

It is not clear whether all of the above arguments have merit. Despite years of foreign investment, the living conditions for Blacks have not improved markedly and the gap between Blacks and whites has not narrowed—even though in absolute terms Blacks may do better, and in relative terms the ratio of Black to white wages may have been reduced slightly. Western investment tends to be in capital-intensive industries, thereby reducing the impact on Black employment.

Black African Opinions on Disinvestment

Nor is it clear where Black South Africans stand on **disinvestment.** Most of the organizations involved in the mass democratic and Black Consciousness movements, organizations believed to be well supported among the politicized segments of the population, favor disinvestment. The most articulate Black voices—those of Bishop Desmond Tutu, Nelson Mandela, the Reverend Allan Boesak, and many others—have been raised in support of this camp. By contrast, some large and politically conservative organizations, including many homeland leaders (e.g., Chief Buthelezi) and fundamentalist church groups, oppose disinvestment. Indeed, it was for many years a criminal offense for South Africans to advocate disinvestment, so it is hard to tell what people are thinking. Public opinion surveys seem to present conflicting data. On the basis of several studies conducted in late 1984 and early 1985, for instance, it was widely believed that around 75 percent of urban Blacks opposed disinvestment and sanctions.

Moderate and conservative politicians in the West have been keen to broadcast these findings in defense of their governments' reticence to call for more activist measures against Pretoria. The South African government and business community seemed, for once, to be willing to argue that Black perspectives should be heeded on this question.

A more comprehensive survey—one that went beyond the dichotomous question, "Is disinvestment a good thing or a bad thing?"—was conducted among Black adults in all ten metropolitan areas in September 1985.[4] A three-way choice was offered, including the category of conditional investment, in which foreign firms can invest only if they actively pressure government to end apartheid. When this third option was offered, fully 49 percent of the sample supported conditional investment, 26 percent favored encouraging all investment, and 24 percent wanted no investment at all. Thus the case could be made that 73 percent favored disinvestment when companies are not working to end apartheid. When efforts were made to determine how far Blacks were prepared to suffer the still-unknown effects of disinvestment (assuming that disinvestment contributes to unemployment and economic slowdown), about a quarter were "hard-line" and advocated disinvestment whatever the cost. Another quarter would support disinvestment if a few, but not many, jobs were to be lost. The remaining half were cautious if sacrifice were involved. The ordinary Black person is implacably hostile to apartheid and willing to hasten its demise, yet, as a wage-earner with dependents, is aware that survival would not be easy without a job.

The Impact of the Debate

Opponents of disinvestment fancy themselves pragmatists. Look, they say, it won't work! Foreign investment represents less than 10 percent of the direct investment in South Africa and less than 20 percent of indirect investment. Unless all major foreign investors together pull out, the impact will be marginal. In that case, opponents ask, why should we bear inordinate costs in a futile gesture? Even if multilateral disinvestment were practical, it is hard to see the causal link between the economic pressure it would create and an appropriate political response from either Pretoria or the Black masses. On the contrary, they say, economic growth will create new jobs, produce better wages as corporations compete for a skilled work force, require the training and promotion of Blacks, and thereby narrow the racial gap. In their view, this is the kind of pressure that forces an end to apartheid—rapid growth, not retrenchment. But their case has not been proven over time.

A number of U.S. organizations—the American Committee on Africa, the Interfaith Center on Corporate Responsibility, the Washington Office on Africa, the American Friends Service Committee, and Trans-Africa, among others—have lobbied and worked at local, state, and national levels to generate support for disinvestment.[5] African-Americans, campus activists, and diverse religious organizations have added to the effort. Slowly, public opinion in the United States began to exhibit approval of more direct private and governmental efforts to force South Africa to change. Among their weapons were resolutions at corporate annual general meetings, demonstrations, disclosures of labor-management practices, boycotts of products of firms in South Africa, picketing of corporate facilities, and employee threats to refuse to work on South African-related projects. Collectively, all have been part of an eductional campaign to apprise Americans of the realities of apartheid and of their own or their organizations' complicity in the system. In this enterprise they have been aided by extensive media coverage of protests and police repression in South Africa as well as of demonstrations in the United States.

As the 1980s wore on, pressures on companies operating in South Africa intensified. Universities, trade unions, and state and local governments divested themselves and their pension funds of holdings in corporations in South Africa. In addition, legislation was passed preventing such corporations from bidding on public service contracts in the United States. Increasingly, U.S. firms faced the possibility of losing American business because they refused to abandon a shrinking South African market. The frustrations of corporate officers became evident. The "hassle factor," as some called it, was consuming too much of their time and that of their boards of directors. More than half the U.S. firms with direct investments in South Africa withdrew between 1984 and 1989. As of 1991, more than 120 U.S. companies still have subsidiaries or investments in operations there. Some 176 companies, about half the total that have departed, have retained ties (licensing, patent, and export arrangements) that do not include equity ownership.[6] Still, an aroused U.S. citizenry, or at least a militant and engaged segment of it, had effectively leveled economic sanctions at South Africa, virtually bypassing the foreign policy machinery of the U.S. government. Although many European firms were also forced to disinvest (e.g., Barclays Bank) and to reconsider their involvement, the impact of the campaign to isolate South Africa was not nearly so compelling in Europe.

The powerful international reaction to the widespread popular uprising from 1984 to 1986 was especially effective in the banking world. As the end of 1986 neared, South Africa was increasingly being cut off from international capital markets. The availability of commercial credits for South African imports was curtailed, even when, as in the case of the U.S. Comprehensive Anti-Apartheid Act of 1986, such trade financing was generally exempt from the prohibitions imposed by Congress. U.S. commercial letters of credit sunk from $123 million in 1983 to $11 million in 1987. Nonbank credits were virtually halved over the same period.[7]

Similarly new capital was cut back drastically. This action combined with the departure of foreign capital previously within the South African economy, forced Pretoria to rethink its policies. International banks began to recall their outstanding short-term loans to South African borrowers. Where could South Africans turn for capital? Alternative sources tapped in the past were drying up. As a result of the loan repayments and the absence of new loans to offset the outflow, between 1984 and 1987 South Africa had a cumulative loss of over $4 billion.[8] The total loss of capital from all sources during the same period was more than twice as large, perhaps as much as $10 billion in current dollar figures.[9]

This loss of capital had a devastating effect on the South African economy because it shut down any prospect for economic growth; without growth, pressures in the Black community were bound to mount. A figure no less important than Nelson Mandela was surprised by the determination of the international banking community: "I did not expect such massive support from bankers. But when it did come, it pleased me very much. Because it was an indication of the impact which the A.N.C. and other political organizations had made on the international community."[10] As a result of the mood and the pressure in question, most of the governments in industrialized Western countries were forced to put in place regulations prohibiting new investment in South Africa and constraints on the flow of capital to South Africa.

CODES OF CONDUCT

Such divestment campaigns, in turn, prompted a device that had the effect of preempting the call for disinvestment. Instituted were numerous codes of conduct, designed to require foreign firms operating in South Africa to establish policies that are more socially responsible toward their Black South African employees and the communities in which they operate.

In 1974, a subcommittee of Britain's House of Commons devised an employment Code of Practice for British firms in South Africa—a code that grew out of revelations in *The Guardian* of substandard wages and working conditions. That Code, in turn, served as the basis for a Code of Conduct adopted by the European Community in 1977. European Political Cooperation, a formal supranational process by which member-states seek to coordinate their foreign policies, sought at that time to develop a common front against apartheid. The European Code emphasized trade union rights in South Africa, enjoined employers to allow employees the freedom to choose organizations to represent them, and urged employers to recognize those bodies. Among the other provisions were recommendations that employers initially pay 50 percent above the minimum subsistence level, try to offset the negative effects of migratory labor, give equal pay for equal work, promote African advancement by introducing training schemes, fund Black education and other benefits, desegregate work places, and publish detailed annual reports on their progress in applying the Code.

From 1977 to 1984, the Code of Conduct was the European Community's sole common foreign policy instrument for promoting change in South Africa. Its provisions sought to negate apartheid labor legislation. Yet the diversity of the Community serves to undermine the Code as a collective policy. Each state retains complete autonomy over monitoring the compliance of its firms. Although the Code is uniformly applicable (on a voluntary basis) to all Community-based firms with subsidiaries operating in South Africa, no Community institution is responsible for central supervision or coordination of the Code, no common reporting format exists, and only one member, the United Kingdom, has submitted annual reports for each year of the Code's existence.

In November 1985, in response to widespread violence, the Community revised the Code to place greater emphasis on relations with Black trade unions (in order to supplement benefits, training, and promotion) and on improving coordination in applying the Code. In spite of these minor revisions, the Code is widely discredited as ineffective. South Africa's post-1984 violence required a more comprehensive and vigorous European Community policy. But the Code was too passive; and its coordination, nil.

In the United States, companies under pressure to withdraw from South Africa or to "do something" to combat apartheid adopted their own voluntary code. At the time, the 350 U.S. firms with facilities in South Africa employed approximately 100,000 workers, 70,000 of whom were Black. The incomes of these workers, in turn, sustained about 300,000 Blacks. If, as the companies claimed, they tended to pay more than local wage norms, then the actions of U.S. firms had wide ramifications on the labor market.

In March 1977, the Reverend Leon H. Sullivan, a Black clergyman and member of the board of General Motors, proposed a voluntary code of conduct that came to be known as the Sullivan Principles. Many of its provisions were derived from the British and European Community codes, although Sullivan's principles stressed desegregation whereas the Community Code emphasized trade union rights. Equally important, whereas the Community governments adopted their Code, the U.S. government had nothing to do with the Sullivan Principles. They were a corporate response to the mounting cries for action against apartheid. Many corporations saw them as a device to obviate governmental action and to defuse a growing public relations problem. Washington supported and encouraged the principles but refused to make them mandatory or to link Eximbank credits to formal observance of the main principles. What is more, some institutional investors have used corporate compliance with the principles as a criterion for decisions regarding divestment of their portfolio holdings.

With the prior endorsement of twelve large firms, Sullivan's six principles soon gained wide acceptance. By 1979, 135 firms had adopted and were applying them with varying degrees of conviction. These principles were as follows:

1. non-segregation at all work facilities;
2. equal and fair employment practices;
3. equal pay for equal work;
4. training programs to prepare Blacks for supervisory, administrative, clerical, and technical jobs;
5. an increased number of Blacks in management and supervisory positions; and
6. improvement in the quality of employees' lives outside the work environment in areas such as housing, transportation, schooling, recreation, and health facilities.

In 1978, Sullivan added the requirement that signatory companies support "the elimination of discrimination against the rights of blacks to form or belong to government-registered trade unions, and to acknowledge generally the right of black workers to form their own unions or to be registered by trade unions where unions already exist." In 1979, companies were required to "assist in the development of black and non-white business enterprises, including distributors, suppliers of goods and services and manufacturers." Corporations were also asked to lobby Pretoria to end not only numerous discriminatory practices but migratory labor practices as well. Corporate progress on these principles was monitored by a private council of signatory companies and a private consulting firm. "Report cards" were issued periodically to individual firms regarding their compliance.

The Sullivan Principles and other codes have been criticized by progressive activists as ineffective and "reformist" (to them a disparaging epithet). Even the South African government approved of the final draft. Reformists in the NP secretly urged signatory companies to push their desegregation efforts harder in order to enable government to make what they felt were manageable changes under pressure from abroad. But the fact is that these codes have proven irrelevant to fundamental changes in apartheid. They were well-meaning, perhaps, and they did provide some leverage; but at heart they diverted activists from their divestment, disinvestment, and sanctions agendas.

Sullivan himself became disillusioned and in May 1985 declared that if apartheid were not ended in two years, he would work for the withdrawal of all U.S. firms and an economic embargo against Pretoria. In June 1987, his threat became reality. He called for total U.S. disinvestment, for an embargo, and for breaking off diplomatic relations with Pretoria. As Pretoria was not prepared to end apartheid on its own, Sullivan maintained, the United States must be prepared to press more actively for change.

THE SOUTH AFRICAN BUSINESS COMMUNITY

At present, the South African business community, especially its financial, mining, and conglomerate components, is concerned that South Africa's further isolation might weaken if not destroy their own operations. These giant firms (some 80 percent of all businesses listed on the Johannesburg stock exchange are controlled by four large conglomerates) are trying to push government along the road to reform. The costs of maintaining an unpopular apartheid state are burdensome. Taxes to sustain the security apparatus, deteriorating labor-management relations, the inefficient use of a poorly prepared labor force, the general unease of operating in a siege economy cut off from technological innovation, capital inflows at reasonable rates and access to foreign markets, and the fear of becoming "captured" by or even identified with government and the NP—all spell trouble for big business.

Yet the NP is increasingly a party representing big business. The 1982 split in the NP restructured the class basis of the party: The Conservative Party siphoned off blue-collar and some middle-class whites and left the NP to the upper-middle, professional, and capital elements of Afrikanerdom. The split also enabled the NP to appeal more directly to English-speaking interests, including pragmatists in the business world.

What the NP government failed to do with the business establishment at its high-profile Carlton and Good Hope conferences in 1979 and 1981—that is, to enlist the predominantly English-speaking business elite in support of NP policy—may have been accomplished by the Conservatives. By abandoning the NP, Conservative Party supporters transformed the NP, pushed it toward the center, and prompted it to adopt, unabashedly, a policy of reform and economic growth, even at the cost of loosening the apartheid chains. Of course, none of this would have been necessary or possible had the Black opposition to minority rule been quiescent or had the outside world acquiesced to blatant white dominance. The NP government was pushed hard to make adjustments.

As English and Afrikaner capital became intertwined, the state increasingly sought to enlist the economic clout and international connections of big business for its political and foreign policy ends. The current NP policy of "privatization," by which the state divests itself of holdings in parastatal corporations (e.g., steel, transport, harbors, the media, electricity, and water), is the culmination of that "free" market/ capitalist mentality. The symbiotic relationship between indigenous business and the state has been discredited and hence abandoned. What the private sector denounces as "state socialism" is slowly being dismantled by the NP government. With these new opportunities and efforts to liberalize labor relations and alter the economy to enable industry to hire the best work force on free market terms, an increasingly concentrated corporate community sees its interests as bound up in a peaceful integration of moderate Black political leadership into central state mechanisms. But it also distributes state assets to private, almost exclusively wealthy white purchasers. Black radicals complain that privatization deprives a future majoritarian government of control of a major economic lever with which it might restructure the economy.

In its day, apartheid served the business community well. It provided an inexpensive work force that was forcefully kept in its "place." But as South Africa's economy became more complex and sophisticated, the old migratory labor arrangements and artificial restrictions against Black acquisition of skills and promotion no longer served business efficiently. South African business saw the need to push government to reform, and fast. The costs of apartheid were too high—and the risks unacceptable.

ECONOMIC SANCTIONS

The Range of Sanctions Options

The range of economic tools available to private groups abroad is limited, largely because their utilization demands massive organization and coordination. Just as important, once such tools are used, their leverage may be short-lived. The threat of disinvestment, for example, is sometimes more telling than the act itself. For economic levers to be successful in forcing governmental changes and in assisting the reformers and revolutionaries, the cumulative effect of hundreds, indeed thousands, of individual decisions—to boycott selected purchases, to vote shares a certain way, to withdraw funds from designated banks, and to ostracize athletes and celebrities who perform in South Africa—must be felt as one. The list is extensive; the impact unclear. For these reasons, it is tempting to try for a quick fix, to enlist the aid and authority of governments, at various levels, to mandate policy changes toward South Africa.

The concept of sanctions is multifaceted and can be confusing. In a larger, generic sense, sanctions are any form of official diplomatic, military, or economic policy that seeks to deny or reduce contacts between the target government and the outside world and thereby either coerce the target regime into changing policy or weaken that regime in order to aid its opponents. For our purposes we shall consider sanctions more narrowly. We shall focus on economic sanctions, the attempt to punish or coerce a state by the severance or closure of economic links and exchanges with the outside world. As such, sanctions can be enacted multilaterally by international organizations and groups of states or unilaterally by one or more states individually; they can also be enacted by substate political entities such as cities, states, and counties in the United States, or even privately by corporations, private organizations, and individual citizens.

Sanctions can be expressed in many ways, through either comprehensive or selective stoppages of trade, investment, infrastructural links (i.e., land, sea, and air communications), financial transfers, loans, and credit. The application of sanctions in any particular case involves a politico-economic decision within a legal as well as a moral context. The basic elements are political purpose and will. The basic tools are economic. The problem is how to influence the political will of the target government and its leaders, or how to weaken them so that they are unable to maintain the regime without significant reform. But no one can be sure in advance exactly what impact each proposed action will have on the actors involved.

The Confusing Debate over Sanctions

The debate in the United States over economic sanctions against South Africa has been long and divisive. In part, it is being waged over the very meaning of sanctions. Some Americans are willing to support partial or minor sanctions. Some want comprehensive sanctions. For many there is confusion over who the sanctioning body should be. Throughout the country, in various private and public venues, Americans have worried over the many facets of this complicated issue. The same debate is being played out throughout the industrialized West as governments and citizens ponder the extent to which economic association with South Africa strengthens or weakens the apartheid regime and the possible effectiveness of various forms of sanctions. At this juncture, then, a brief summary of the issues would be helpful. We must beware, however, of the dangers of oversimplifying the highly speculative and sometimes subjective claims involved.

First, the goals of sanctions are often unclear and contradictory. Short of a common desire to bring an end to apartheid, advocates of sanctions have diverse purposes and motivations. Some perceive apartheid as evil and thus consider support for sanctions to be a moral imperative. Even if sanctions do not achieve the demise of apartheid, they contend, it is important to do what is morally right and to end one's complicity with Pretoria. Others see sanctions as a way of expressing their support for Black southern Africans, particularly those who risk their lives resisting apartheid rule. Many on the political left see sanctions as a blow against capitalism—both within South Africa and throughout the world. Because they believe that the capitalist world perpetuates racism and exploitation in South Africa, they favor any effort to devitalize these capitalist links.

Far more common and less ideological is the view that sanctions will have the effect of raising the costs of maintaining apartheid. Of course, there is a punitive dimension to this argument. By depriving Pretoria and its white constituency of valued goods or by embarrassing and shaming them, sanctions, it is hoped, would result in a loss of internal support for the regime. But it is not easy to invoke selective sanctions to target those most responsible for or benefiting inordinately from apartheid. The more general the sanctions, the more likely the Black masses will suffer. The question of whether these vulnerable people are prepared to endure even greater economic hardship in the vague hope that the regime will surrender or modify its policies is indeed a contentious issue.

The most popular Black leaders in South Africa, Nelson Mandela and Bishop Desmond Tutu among them, call for strengthened sanctions. They say that although Blacks suffer from sanctions, they are prepared to make the material sacrifices necessary to end an even greater suffering, that which is brought on by racism and exploitation. In fact, all major Black political movements, trade unions, and church groups in South Africa (with the exception of Inkatha) advocate sanctions to end apartheid. Nonetheless, former Prime Minister Margaret Thatcher, for example, insists that sanctions hurt Blacks the most and thus, ostensibly, did not merit her support. Using this excuse, Great Britain lifted some sanctions (which had never been vigorously enforced by the Conservative government) after Mandela was released in February 1990.

For some perhaps cynical or "hard-nosed" sanctioneers, Black suffering is a key concern. To them, sanctions are a form of economic warfare that, when they work, drive people to desperation. The masses are expected to suffer and then to rise up against their oppressors. There will be bloodshed and hardship, they contend, but "you can't make an omelet without breaking eggs." As sanctions pinch the oppressed, the oppressor is also pinched and becomes less and less able to mount the effort necessary to defend the system. After all, many South Africans have taken up arms against the government. They have signaled their preparedness to risk their lives for self-rule. Still others in the sanctioning state support sanctions in the belief that this policy will be well received elsewhere in Black Africa and the Third World. Sanctions are thus a symbol of a desire for better relations with the less-developed world. A state's policy toward South Africa thereby becomes instrumental to other facets of its foreign policy.

Almost all advocates of sanctions assume that comprehensive economic sanctions will bring down the apartheid regime only when they are employed in concert with other pressures on the regime. Few are clear about the sequence or character of the transition to a postapartheid order.

Is South Africa Vulnerable to Sanctions?

We cannot be sure of the logic implicit in this strategy. Much of it is based on guesswork or on economic measures of impact that are debatable and often challenged. It is fairly clear that sanctions will bring on economic hardship. That is what they are designed to do. But hardship for whom? And will that hardship, in concert with other pressures on the regime (sabotage, diplomacy, political mobilization, work stoppages, and so forth) so weaken the resolve of the minority government that it would consider alternative power arrangements? The literature seems to cast doubt on the hope that sanctions alone can bring about the political or psychological collapse of a regime.[11]

Analysts often use the example of Rhodesia to argue that sanctions will not work against South Africa. But the Rhodesian model is not necessarily analogous, nor can one say unequivocally that sanctions failed to bring down the white regime in Rhodesia. Although there is evidence that sanctions initially steeled white intransigence to domestic political change,[12] the long-term effects of sanctions coupled with protracted guerrilla war eventually brought down the Smith government. In that respect, it could be argued that sanctions "worked," but slowly. Economic isolation did, after all, contribute to Rhodesia's vulnerability to largely internal military resistance. The same outcome could conceivably apply to South Africa as well.

The South African economy is externally oriented. Its dependence upon trade with, and technology and investment from, the West is apparent. Exports are largely of raw materials and gold. Imports are increasingly of capital goods crucial to the operation of industry and mining. Because imports outpace exports, foreign capital is vital to the system. Loans, credits, and investments are the lubricants without which the economy would falter. The financial sanctions growing out of South Africa's 1985 debt crisis had a devastating effect on the country's financial reputation. Its balance and terms of trade were compromised, its import purchasing power suffered, and the value of the rand plummeted. South Africa's financial situation fell into serious disarray.

But does this mean that sanctions could cause hardship so severe that the regime would seek relief by altering its policies? And could the hardship be lessened, for a price, by companies and governments prepared to profit from South Africa's predicament?

The answers lie partly in the types of sanctions being discussed.[13] Trade sanctions and capital sanctions are those most commonly considered and are partially in force today. Many analysts who have studied the South African economy have concluded that South Africa's vulnerability ties in with its need to import capital goods. As capital goods are the engines of further growth, serious economic relocations would be imperative in their absence. But there is little sense that the slowdown would happen overnight.

Efforts to prevent South African exports from reaching world markets are more problematic. Nevertheless, a stoppage of exports was the emphasis recommended by a panel of experts in a report prepared in July 1989 for the Commonwealth Committee of Foreign Ministers on Southern Africa.[14] But given the strategic importance of South Africa's minerals and gold, always in high demand and relatively easy to ship and disguise, the cessation of exports would be difficult. Moreover, as the main end of exports is to gain foreign exchange in order to buy capital goods (including computers), it stands to reason that the focus should be on preventing imports of capital goods. The Commonwealth panel, however, felt that South Africa's immediate need is for foreign exchange to pay off large bank debts. Thus, it reasoned, a cutoff of exports would work quickly. In the past, advocates of sanctions called for an oil embargo against South Africa, but Pretoria took steps (with the aid of foreign-based engineering and petroleum companies) to rectify that deficiency. Today, analysts feel that an oil cutoff would not be so effective.

Clearly, the threat of comprehensive sanctions worries the South African authorities and business community.[15] They have taken measures, at some considerable expense, to reduce their vulnerabilities in the areas of energy and weapons. They have sought to construct an elaborate network of shadow organizations by which to overcome embargoes.[16] They have tried to develop key industries so as to enhance their self-sufficiency in times of embargo. Petroleum is a case in point. For years it was assumed that South Africa would be vulnerable to an oil embargo inasmuch as it produced no petroleum of its own. Estimates indicate that in the decade after 1973, when OPEC boycotted sales to South Africa, the country spent some $10 billion extra as a premium to ensure supplies—a significant sum equivalent to South Africa's entire foreign debt in 1985. The embargo forced the government to concentrate on creating substitute gasoline supplies by means of an expensive coal-to-petroleum process developed by a parastatal corporation, Sasol. Sanctions, in this specific case, took a heavy economic toll, even though they were successfully bypassed.[17]

During the 1970s, South Africa was able to take advantage of what amounted to a windfall capital injection. Gold was and is South Africa's most important export. In the late 1960s and early 1970s, gold's position on the free market strengthened—so much so that, with mounting U.S. trade deficits, pressure on the U.S. dollar sharpened. The gold price had been fixed at $35 an ounce for forty years. In 1971, speculation against the dollar and into gold mounted. The United States decided to allow gold to find its own value, thereby effectively abandoning the gold standard. By June 1972, the price of gold had risen to $60. Then the dollar was devalued. By the end of 1974, gold stood at $198. Eventually it sailed to more than $400 an ounce. The inflated price of gold served to salvage a faltering South African economy. It has been estimated that during the 1970s, every $10 increase on the average annual price of gold meant an increase of 1 percent in South Africa's GNP. Gold provided a hedge against hard times. Even with a falling output, South Africa's economy managed to prosper.

Furthermore, South Africans have lobbied and worked abroad to outflank the advocates of sanctions. They have come to realize that the days of bluster are over. Comprehensive sanctions are a serious threat, especially if enough businesses and governments are willing to comply with and enforce measures to isolate South Africa economically. Sanctions may not bring Pretoria to its knees, and they certainly will not take effect in a matter of months. But they can be costly, and South Africa's power elite does fear their more thorough imposition. If the international community is brought to consider seriously widening and enforcing sanctions, enough powerful actors would clearly also be searching for other ways to supplement the pressure on Pretoria. In short, sanctions, along with other critical steps, would spell the end to apartheid. As sanctions begin to take effect, well-off and mobile whites might look carefully for opportunities to emigrate—resulting in a slow hemorrhage of capital and skills rather than a panic flight. A similar sequence took place in Rhodesia.

Before negotiations took place with the ANC, the Western industrial countries had been edging toward more and more complete sanctions. Part of the problem in putting sanctions in place is that some advocates of sanctions want them on the cheap. They want Pretoria to suffer without making serious sacrifices themselves. Clearly the burden of enforcing sanctions would fall unevenly on the sanctioning country. If, for example, restrictions were to be placed on the import of South African chromium, or vanadium, or manganese, the steel industry would be expected to locate alternate sources of supply and to pay presumably higher prices in a market with reduced supplies and fixed demands. If the decision were made to embargo the export of, say, computer equipment or automobile technology to South Africa, the computer and automotive industries would lose customers. Particular firms would indeed be hit harder than others. Accordingly, governments under pressure to enact sanctions are also under pressure to lift the burden off of politically powerful interests. The usual result is that sanctions which do not hurt the sanctioning country do not hurt the target state either. In any case, ways are eventually devised to evade enforcement.

In September 1986, the foreign ministers of the European Community agreed on a new set of sanctions that banned imports of gold, steel, and gold coins and prohibited new investments by European firms. But enforcement of even these minimum measures has been less than airtight. In October of the same year, the U.S. Congress enacted the Comprehensive Anti-Apartheid Act over President Reagan's veto. The measure banned most new corporate investments and bank loans, prohibited the importation of numerous South African goods (including uranium, coal, steel, iron, textiles and agricultural products, although it excluded some other strategic minerals), and barred U.S. exports of petroleum products and a wider range of weaponry. It also ended U.S. landing rights for South African Airways. Despite the Reagan administration's opposition to sanctions and the legalistic steps by the Reagan and Bush administrations to interpret these provisions very narrowly, a start was made to enforce these provisions. Between 1983 and 1987, U.S. imports from South Africa were reduced by 39 percent and exports to South Africa by 45 percent.[18] Two years later, the House of Representatives passed an even more sweeping package of sanctions, but the legislation failed to gain Senate approval. Under former Prime Minister Thatcher, Great Britain was the most vocal opponent of sanctions among South Africa's Western economic partners.

Yet there is undeniable evidence that even these incomplete sanctions have taken a toll on the South African economy. South Africa admits as much. Both Finance Minister Barend du Plessis and the South African Broadcasting Corporation (often regarded as a government mouthpiece) have credited sanctions with pushing government toward social reform. A 1989 econometric study by the economics division of South Africa's Trust Bank found that since 1985, sanctions and disinvestment had led to a cumulative foreign exchange loss of about $15.21 billion. The indirect impact was far greater than those directly measurable and more visible consequences on specifically targeted industries. Production losses (because of the macro-multiplier effect of $15 billion on GDP) may be about $30.42 billion, and the total spending or "standard of living" loss approaches $38 billion. And as consumer spending is estimated to have decreased by approximately 15 percent because of sanctions, there were about 500,000 fewer jobs than would have been the case without sanctions (i.e., taking into account not only job losses but also the reduced number of jobs created).[19] The overall effect of sanctions has been to discourage long-range development and to create a survival mentality in the economy. In other words, the long-term effect of the political and economic uncertainty related to sanctions has been even greater than the immediate, direct impact.

Advocates of sanctions maintain that sanctions are the nonviolent option in dealing with apartheid. But many have come to realize, especially now that the de Klerk government has taken steps to demonstrate its willingness to negotiate and share power (even though the ANC and NP vocabularies of democracy differ tremendously), that most Western governments are not prepared to launch a coordinated policy to isolate South Africa economically, at least enough to raise the level of economic pain.

The "Free Market" Alternative to Sanctions

For as long as the Pretoria government appears to be open and flexible, the tasks of undermining apartheid from the outside will fall to the champions of supply-side economics. There are plenty of opponents of apartheid who firmly believe (and for some it is an article of faith) that capitalism is a progressive force and that growth and large-scale investment from abroad are the best tonics for improving race relations in South Africa. Inside South Africa this view is associated with Harry Oppenheimer of the Anglo-American Corporation (which is neither English nor American) and Helen Suzman, until recently a long-time liberal member of parliament and opponent of the NP and apartheid. As they see it, economic growth is a liberating force. Because so much of South Africa's economic growth depends on trade and investment from abroad, external inputs become an unqualified good. In the long run, they contend, the ruling elite will have to recognize that continued growth requires the rational use of the factors of production, including all labor, and hence rewards must go to the most efficient suppliers of labor. Opportunity to acquire a skill must be made available to all. A vibrant capitalist economy, based on the free flow of factors and the mechanisms of supply and demand, cannot afford the inefficiencies of apartheid. Therefore, generate economic activity rather than stifle it— that is the key to ending apartheid.

Their fundamental premise, that capitalist economic models inevitably yield an equitable and adequate dispensation for social well-being, has been challenged for years by both Marxist and non-Marxist social scientists and philosophers. Certainly in the South African case, there seems to be little correlation between periods of rapid growth and the breakdown of apartheid structures. Indeed, apartheid became more firmly entrenched during the boom years of the 1950s and 1960s. It also became an important foundation in the government's labor policy. South African industry and externally based corporations adapted well to the social dictates from Pretoria. Indeed, they even found ways to enhance their profits in the process. Advocates of capitalism as an antiapartheid force need a very long perspective, for in the short run—in decades, not centuries—the demands of economic modernization have been manageable and existing institutions of racial superordination have proven to be durable, even in the face of progressive capitalist demands. The business community seems to be liberal, but for conservative ends. In other words it seeks reform and restructuring largely to stabilize the capitalist system and to make South African businesses more competitive. Since World War II, apartheid and modern capitalism have been more than tolerant of one another, and more mutually supportive. The business community, however, would never admit to this supportive relationship. This is not to say that they will remain so in the future. It is merely a piece of historical evidence necessary to understand why radical South Africans reject the argument that capitalism is a progressive force. They are, it would seem, ideologically reluctant to admit that capitalism is capable of adaptation or of monumental reform that might, fortuitously, benefit the Black masses.

CONCLUSION

So the argument over which economic instruments of foreign policy should be employed and how in order to confront apartheid turns on the basic question: Will South Africa respond more acceptably to isolation or to engagement? Those with a direct capital investment in South Africa tend to be advocates of the latter. Few of them were open critics of apartheid until pressures mounted in recent years to do something about it. Coming from them, the assertion that economic involvement in South Africa works to end apartheid is less than convincing. The same people now despair that sanctions may hurt Blacks, even though for years they seldom expressed concern for Black interests. Indeed, many regularly resisted Black demands for improved wages, working conditions, and social changes.

There are exceptions to these generalizations, both within South Africa and abroad. But overall, those benefiting from the status quo as well as those uneasy with Black power tend to call for engagement. A number of people fearful of violence also prefer arguments for gradual or evolutionary change rather than sudden change springing from economic hardship, frustration, and revolution. Westerners who have seen how subtle pressure and reasoned argument work in their own societies prefer a patient, persistent pressure on Pretoria. Isolation, they maintain, severs the links required to exert that pressure; the end of trade and the withdrawal of investments reduce, not increase, the ability of outsiders to influence a regime.

Those favoring isolation are a more disparate lot. Ranging from Communist and Marxist opponents of capitalism and Western involvement in Africa to intellectuals and religious leaders, from ordinary citizens appalled by the excesses of apartheid to trade unionists and Black activists, they have grown impatient with the business-as-usual approach. Thus far, no definitive answer has emerged from this debate. For now, Pretoria seems to have neutralized the advocates of comprehensive sanctions. And the chances for new sanctions are slim, unless the reform process gets off track. Slim, too, are the chances for ending the sanctions currently in place before more tangible changes in the system are brought about.

But the Western powers never were comfortable with limited sanctions and the economic isolation of South Africa. Any serious effort on Pretoria's part to end apartheid and integrate Blacks into the central political order would probably bring about the swift reintegration of South Africa into the global economy (not that it ever was economically isolated). To their credit, many of the ruling elite now understand that the current world mood will not permit unrestrained exploitation and repression of the indigenous majority and, moreover, that the current structure of the economy no longer yields unbridled gain to those who fail to make full use of the intellectual capacities of most citizens.

If a more enlightened South African leadership were to take serious steps to end apartheid and move toward a majoritarian regime, or even one with shared power, South Africa would be permitted to slip back into its role as an intermediary or semiperipheral power. Indeed, South Africa would be well placed at that point to assume a regional leadership role far beyond its aspirations during the apartheid years before the capitalist world became sensitized to or compelled to address the evils of legalized racial domination.

FIVE

□ □ □

Cast Out by a Hostile World Community

S tudents of international relations are familiar with efforts to categorize states according to fundamentally economic factors. The trichotomy of First World (the industrialized, developed, democratic, and largely Western states), Third World (the less-developed, poorer countries of the so-called South), and the increasingly less cohesive and less analytically valid Second World (the socialist states of Europe) is now part of our political vocabulary. Such simple and crude divisions have been supplemented by terms such as the Fourth World of resource-rich though still not economically balanced or militarily strong countries, and the Fifth World, those in abject poverty, the totally vulnerable "basket-cases" with little prospect for economic growth and development. The UN has identified some thirty-one "least developed" of the less-developed countries. There has also emerged, largely on the Pacific rim, another group of **newly industrialized countries** (NICs): their principal resource, a hard-working, disciplined and increasingly skilled labor force.

ISOLATION OR ENGAGEMENT
IN THE DIPLOMATIC ARENA

Such world configurations, stratified along lines of economic promise and performance, tell us little about the distinctive features of cultures, regimes, and policies in these states. So other designations begin to creep into the nomenclature. Yehezkel Dror wrote of "crazy states," a term derived from an analysis of what he regards as irrational state behavior.[1] Dror focused on leaders (not peoples), a contemporary list of whom might include Idi Amin, Mohammar Ghaddafy, and the Ayatollah Khomeini. Elie Wiesel, the Nobel laureate, has also written of the "fear of madness" and the power of the irrational in foreign affairs.

But there are situations more deeply disturbing than mere leadership deficiencies. There is a class of states that trouble large portions of the collective conscience of mankind. They pose problems more intractable than can be addressed simply by removing a head of government who is unpredictable, irrational, or downright criminal or psychotic. These regimes have been accorded labels such as outcast, outlaw, pariah, and leper.[2] To all but their apologists, they are embarrassments the world would like to see evaporate, without further strife or bloodshed. These are regimes that, by their genesis, their ideologies, their demeanor, or their compound deeds, so violate our moral precepts that we are prepared to remove them, physically if necessary, or to banish them from the normal commerce of statehood. So offensive are these regimes that they are both outcasts and in danger of being cast out, insofar as that is possible, by the formal actions of governments and institutions that presume to articulate world opinion and universal norms.

The world community acts by the cumulative decisions of individual governments. Pariahhood is a condition brought on by the nature of state order, compounded by the state's determination not to conform to ostensibly universal social standards and expectations. There is no hard and fast set of symptoms or indices by which to indentify an outcast regime. No state is totally abandoned. There are degrees of rejection. Indeed, it is possible for an outcast regime to play an active role in the world, especially in economic or military terms. According to my subjective reckoning, the following states would fall into the outcast category—Rhodesia during the fifteen years of "independence" under white rule (1965 to 1980); Kampuchea under Pol Pot after 1975; Taiwan since its withdrawal from the UN in 1971; and the so-called independent national states, or homelands, created by South Africa. At various times and under various circumstances Israel, Iran, Iraq, and Cuba have also been called outcasts. South Africa itself, since 1948, had drifted closer to outcast status and, in the eyes of many (if not most) of the actors in world affairs, deserves that designation.

Despite the almost universally reviled nature of the South African regime, there is considerable debate over how best to deal with the government in Pretoria. Diplomacy along with economic intercourse are two powerful levers by which to influence governments and their peoples. As in the economic arena, the debate goes on in diplomatic circles as to how change in South Africa can be most effectively prompted or forced. The question of engagement versus isolation is reiterated in this forum, too. In this diplomatic problem, governmental officials are the agents of regular contact and official government-to-government pressure. But the engagement/isolation debate also touches on the issue of private contacts with South Africa, among artists, athletes, entertainers, academics, and religious communicants.

AT THE UNITED NATIONS

Perhaps the ultimate expressions of the isolationist perspective are the various efforts to exclude and expel South Africa from international organizations.[3] Advocates of these actions hope to place South Africa beyond the pale, as a pariah in the world community. The very act of isolation indicates that South Africa's apartheid is not acceptable in a civil world order. Ostracization is designed both to humiliate and to punish Pretoria. A government that is no longer a full participant in the global community will eventually have to mend its ways, so the argument runs, for the costs of survival in a diplomatic version of solitary confinement will escalate beyond tolerance.

Early in its existence it was the intention of the Organization of African Unity to try to exclude South Africa from the UN. Almost from its creation in May 1963, the OAU sought to decolonize southern Africa. Decolonization, in fact, was the second item (after drafting the charter) on the agenda of the summit meeting at which the OAU was founded. The very first resolution adopted by that august conference and reaffirmed at the first ordinary session of the Assembly of Heads of State and Government (the supreme organ of the OAU) in Cairo in July 1964 defined the role of the OAU in the liberation of southern Africa. Among other things, that resolution called on member-states to break off diplomatic and consular relations with the governments of Portugal (still a colonial power at the time) and South Africa, and to boycott all trade with those countries. At subsequent OAU meetings of foreign ministers and heads of state and government, these calls were repeated and sharpened. But although the African governments (with one key exception) conformed to the diplomatic mandate, they were unable by either example or argument to persuade all governments outside of Africa to sever their ties with Pretoria. Indeed, when Malawi and South Africa established diplomatic relations on December 10, 1967, the OAU's uncompromising stand against dealing with South Africa was shattered. H. Kamuzu Banda's decision to open diplomatic relations with South Africa was widely criticized in the OAU. Zambia even requested that Malawi be expelled from the organization. But that proposal failed because there was no clause in the OAU charter regarding expulsion of a member-state.

In 1963 alone, two Security Council special meetings were held to discuss the demand by the African states that South Africa and Portugal be expelled from the UN. These demands eventually led to calls for an end to sales of military materiel to South Africa and for other international embargoes, but the effort to expel South Africa had already been successfully blunted by the Western permanent members of the Security Council.

The General Assembly (directly and through its Committee on Credentials) has rejected since 1973 the credentials of the South African delegation and has thereby denied South Africa its seat. In fact, the Assembly did not go so far as to eject South Africa in 1973. Rather, it promised action in subsequent years. When Pretoria saw that the Africans had an easy majority in 1974, they decided to withdraw. The Assembly took the symbolic step of excluding South Africa from participation in the 1974 session. Pretoria retained its delegation to the UN, but its ambassador did not attempt to take its seat in the General Assembly except when the Namibia question was debated. Representatives of African governments since 1974 have demanded South Africa's expulsion from the General Assembly.[4] But we should note that the UN Charter provides that the rights and privileges of membership be suspended by the General Assembly on the Security Council's recommendation when preventative or enforcement action has been taken against the member (Art. 5), that a member that is a persistent violator of Charter principles may be expelled by the General Assembly on the Security Council's recommendation (Art. 6), and that any member two or more years in arrears in its financial contribution to the organization may be deprived of its vote by the General Assembly. However, South Africa's credentials were rejected by the General Assembly without a recommendation to that effect by the Security Council.

Clearly, South Africa enjoyed the protection of the Great Powers, by their use of their vetoes as permanent members of the Security Council. But an additional reason for South Africa's survival at the UN is that many opponents of apartheid are not entirely convinced that South Africa's banishment is the wise course. Many feel that they could exert more pressure on Pretoria with South Africa inside the UN rather than outside it. Finally, a number of member-states are committed to the principle of universality for this international organization. The memory of the fragmentation of the League of Nations, either because some key states never joined or because others abandoned or felt forced to withdraw from the organization, still lingers. Some members have thus sought to include all states and to have no "tests" for participation. Before South Africa's membership in the UN organization was seriously challenged,

African governments pressed their campaign against South Africa in other UN organs.

The first UN affiliate to express strong disapproval of South Africa was the UN Educational, Scientific, and Cultural Organization (UNESCO). In the early 1950s, that body published reports critical of apartheid. At first, the South African government tried to persuade UNESCO to alter its views and practices but, failing in that endeavor, announced its withdrawal in protest. South Africa's pattern, followed for years, was to withdraw from a UN body rather than endure the ignominy of expulsion.

Africans also succeeded in forcing South Africa to withdraw from the Food and Agriculture Organization in 1963 and from the International Labor Organization and World Health Organization (WHO) in 1964. The International Civil Aviation Organization and the International Telecommunications Union later took steps to force South Africa's withdrawal. In these instances, considerable determination was needed to win their case. The usual procedure, which included the introduction of motions to exclude South Africa, often prompted sharp disagreements with Western delegations. The International Labor Conference, for example, had to be adjourned for a few days to allow the delegates to calm down. At that point South Africa withdrew. African delegations boycotted the 1963 WHO meeting following a confrontation between the Africans and Britain, France, and South Africa. The following year, after the Africans had submitted a draft resolution to deny South Africa a vote in the proceedings, South Africa took the hint and withdrew both from the session and from the organization.

Down the line, coincidental and coordinated action took place at regional and specialized agencies. When the UN Regional Cartographic Conference for Africa opened in Nairobi in July 1963, for example, no one from South Africa appeared. It was later revealed that the Kenyan government had declared any South Africa delegates to be prohibited immigrants. In other words, unlike the other delegates, South Africans would receive no visas on request at the Nairobi airport.[5] This device was used elsewhere in Africa, at such other organizations as the UN Economic Commission for Africa, the Commission for Technical Cooperation in Africa, and the Scientific Council for Africa.

But the Africans and other Third World governments were not successful in all cases. Their efforts to expel South Africa from the Universal Postal Union (UPU) came to naught. They forced South Africa out of the Congress of the UPU, but not out of the Union itself. South Africa still cooperates with that body.

The African tactics were parried at the International Atomic Energy Agency (IAEA). Interestingly, South Africa had been instrumental in the formation of the IAEA and in developing its first safeguards system. In turn, South Africa found the IAEA membership to be of value, inasmuch as it gave Pretoria access to the latest information on nuclear science and technology. Not only were the Africans in the minority among the IAEA membership, but most Western members realized that if South Africa were no longer a member, Pretoria would be free to ignore the IAEA regulations and restrictions with regard to nuclear development and experimentation. The Africans were unable to press their position beyond forcing South Africa's removal from its seat on the prestigious IAEA Board of Governors in June 1977, a position it had held responsibly since the Board's inception in 1957. The credentials of the South African delegation to the General Conference were rejected in 1979. And in 1981, South Africa was removed from the Committee on Assurance of Supply. It has also been denied technical assistance from the IAEA. As recently as 1987, the Third World states pressed for the expulsion of South Africa from the IAEA. But in a well-timed announcement, President Botha stated in September 1987 that his government was prepared to open talks with the nuclear powers about signing the **Non-Proliferation Treaty** (NPT). A few days later both the United States and the Soviet Union delegations to the IAEA opposed the move against South Africa. The Third World initiative failed. Nevertheless, South Africa still participates in the World Bank and the International Monetary Fund, albeit in secondary roles and under considerable pressure. And it is active in other international organizations where African and Asian states have a lesser voice, as in the case of scientific cooperation under the Antarctic Treaty and the International Whaling Convention.

THE COMMONWEALTH OF NATIONS

The Union of South Africa had been one of the early and enthusiastic members of the British Commonwealth of Nations.[6] But the character of the Commonwealth began to change in the 1950s. Before World War II, it was just a club-like gathering of dominions populated by kith and kin from the British imperial diaspora. South Africa was something of an ethnic but not racial exception inasmuch as its government was controlled by a coalition of English-speakers and Afrikaners who favored or at least acquiesced to the imperial ideal and dominated a population the overwhelming majority of whom were Black Africans. After the war, the Commonwealth began to welcome governments from newly independent ex-colonies in Asia and Africa. With each passing year, the atmosphere at Commonwealth conferences became more unfriendly toward South Africa as the organization became more racially diverse.

The new members were vocal and active in their opposition to apartheid and in their advocacy of decolonization and racial dignity.

This trend was heightened in 1960. At the time of the March 1960 Sharpeville demonstration and its bloody aftermath, there was talk of expelling South Africa from the Commonwealth. At the May 1960 Prime Ministers' Conference in London, the South African representative had indicated that his country would hold a referendum on republicanism later that year. He asked for approval in advance of its continued membership in the Commonwealth. This request was similar to but not the same as requests previously granted to India, Pakistan, and Ceylon; indeed, it was much like the request that Ghana made successfully at the same meeting. In these cases the requests came after governments had taken decisions to become republican states, but before the dates of constitutional transition. The Asian and African members saw South Africa's request as an opportunity for a full airing of South Africa's racist policies. Although an agreement was made not to discuss the South African problem at the conference, South Africa's representative did participate in informal discussions about Pretoria's racial order. At the time, however, the matter of the application for continued membership was deemed hypothetical and hence inappropriate in advance of the referendum itself. This awkward issue was bypassed by the Commonwealth's assertion that it did not want to prejudice the forthcoming referendum in South Africa.

Republican status had long been regarded by Afrikaner nationalists as a goal and symbol of their genuine independence from Great Britain and as an end to imperial links that ostensibly made South Africa a less than sovereign state. In the October 1960 referendum, a narrow majority of the largely white electorate, 52 percent, favored the change to republican status. But the new republican constitution changed little on the domestic front. A state president was substituted for the governor-general, although the perceived wrongs of the Anglo-Boer War, of British colonial rule, of the monarchy, and of the juridical need to appeal to a higher authority outside of South Africa were hardly righted in this one symbolic act.

As May 31, 1961, was set for the inauguration of the republic, South Africa applied for continued membership in the Commonwealth to take effect after that date. When that application was considered by the Prime Ministers' Conference in March 1961, several ministers sharply attacked South Africa's racial policies. Whatever support there was for continued membership faded as the meeting progressed. Seeing the writing on the wall, Verwoerd withdrew South Africa's application. Although technically South Africa withdrew from the Commonwealth, in actuality it was expelled. But the expulsion was not an organized or coordinated strategy to isolate South Africa and thereby force it to mend its ways. In fact, there had been considerable hope among the prewar members, even as late as the first session of the 1961 Prime Ministers' Conference, that a formula could be found, that some magic wording for a final communique might be drafted that would allow members to agree to disagree and thereby allow South Africa to continue as a member.

Realistically speaking, this was a diplomatic pipe dream indulged in by some members of the "old" Commonwealth. Several members had indicated that they found South Africa's policies incompatible with membership. Others reserved the right to move for expulsion. Julius Nyerere, the chief minister of a soon-to-be-independent Tanganyika (later Tanzania), broadcast the position that if South Africa were still a member when Tanganyika gained independence, it would not apply to join. Whatever basis there had been for compromise soon evaporated. It was sure to have ended when the flood of new states joined the Commonwealth after 1960.

The NP government was not entirely displeased with being relieved of its symbolic association with a British and increasingly non-Western Commonwealth. Verwoerd's "voluntary" withdrawal enabled Pretoria to retain both its sense of pride and its strong bilateral ties with individual Commonwealth governments. Verwoerd spoke of "freedom" from old colonial masters and outside domination. But there were also "links of advantage"—namely, material benefits that South Africa continued to enjoy. In fact, even after its expulsion, South Africa continued to secure "Commonwealth preferences" in tariffs and trade. It also remained in the sterling area, a group of countries that kept most of their exchange reserves at the Bank of England and in return had access to the London capital and money market. Elements of "special status," especially with the "white Commonwealth," survived the break. From the perspective of Black governments north of the Zambezi, these vestigial survivals of Commonwealth association appeared to be a dangerous Western connivance in the perpetuation of apartheid. They certainly did not help Great Britain's relations with its newer Commonwealth partners.

At home, the South African government rationalized its ostracization from international organizations. It argued that many of these organizations were dominated by immature states, many of them procommunist. It also arrogantly predicted that, in a decade or so, the Western states themselves would abandon the UN and its ancillary organizations and that, after a period of frustration and failure, the newer states would recognize the folly of their ways and come back to a more reasonable line with regard to South Africa.

Most white South Africans accepted Verwoerd's explanation and the debate within South Africa over Commonwealth membership soon died, even among English-speakers who came so close to carrying the republican referendum just a year earlier. Whites seemed to accept Verwoerd's view that "without any hesitation my choice is to have fewer friends and ensure the survival of my Nation." He argued that formal alliances and associations are pointless if your admission to them requires that you renounce the central objective of your government's policy—white supremacy. And he went on to say that "in isolation in the sphere of colour policy lies our strength. If we were to agree to the demands of other Nations because in that sphere we are afraid of the world isolation then we would go under. But isolation in this one sphere does not mean complete isolation. There is a lot of co-operation gained from states in other spheres."[7] Economically, South Africa still had a lot going for it, although Verwoerd, in this case, seemed to be trying to make a virtue of rejection.

Diplomatically, however, the Commonwealth—especially the early members of that organization—are still trying to play a progressive role in South African affairs. They have sought to use the Commonwealth not merely as a body that periodically condemns apartheid and seeks to isolate South Africa, but as a diplomatic lever to urge the South African government to change and, by so doing, to usher a more acceptable South Africa back into the community of nations. It has not been easy. South Africa, especially the SADF and its military intelligence arms, seemed determined and able to undermine the Department of Foreign Affairs' efforts to reconcile South Africa to the larger community.

The events of May 1986 are a good example. At its Nassau summit in 1985, the Commonwealth established a blue-ribbon committee known as the Eminent Persons Group (EPG) on southern Africa.[8] The seven-member EPG was charged with trying to advance the process of change in South Africa. To that end, it traveled to the region in February, March, and May 1986 to take testimony and engage in dialogue with the South African government. Although the EPG was a creative experiment in organizational diplomacy, the ultimate results achieved little. Its efforts were brought to an abrupt end by South Africa's simultaneous military attacks on three Commonwealth capitals—Gaberone, Harare, and Lusaka—on May 19, 1986, the day the EPG was scheduled to leave South Africa. These attacks were South Africa's statement of contempt for the Commonwealth, the EPG, and the process of peaceful resolution. Apparently South Africa was not ready to negotiate either a reduction of its authority or an end to apartheid, and certainly not with outsiders who were meddling in its national affairs.

Since then, Conservative Party governments have steadfastly refused to lend a voice to further Commonwealth efforts to tighten sanctions or to isolate South Africa. In the absence of the U.K.'s support, Commonwealth members are conscious of the organization's limited capacity to influence events in South Africa.

INDIVIDUAL GOVERNMENTAL ACTIONS

Individual governments, too, have taken steps to disengage from and thereby isolate South Africa. Usually they are moved by direct political or partisan pressure at home. Occasionally they may take moderate steps in order to deflect or preempt such pressures. Unilateral actions may also grow from motives of principle and moral conviction. Indeed, the great variety of possible steps has opened a range of policy options only marginally tapped by South Africa's opponents.

From time to time, governments have severed diplomatic relations. They have recalled ambassadors and military and trade attachés to protest specific South African policies. And numerous other bilateral cooperative agreements in the financial, commercial, educational, defense, scientific, and agricultural fields have been reduced or terminated. Here are a few examples. In 1975, Great Britain ended its use of the Simonstown naval facility near Cape Town. During the same year the United States closed down its NASA/Defense Department space tracking facilities near Johannesburg. Moreover, the United States no longer permits its naval vessels to berth in South Africa or its sailors to take shore leave in South African ports. Finally in 1977, the West German government decided to limit export guarantees for business with South Africa.

Some governments have refused to honor South African passports, and some have engaged in visa "wars" with Pretoria. Others, mostly in Africa, have refused to accept citizens of third states if their passports contain visas from South Africa. Tourist travel is discouraged and even banned by some governments, and cultural and educational activities have been terminated. Some citizens have called for their governments to cease all intelligence cooperation (both civil and military) with their counterpart South African agencies. And various reciprocal tax and credit facilities have been withdrawn, thus discouraging present and future investments in South Africa and further reducing South Africa's contacts abroad.

Yet within various governments and bureaucracies, officials and agencies have found ways to undermine these efforts. Britain and the United States still maintain intelligence links with Pretoria. Government agents can thwart sanctions. Financial exhanges continue. Scientific and educational ties are made at official and unofficial levels. If individual bureaucrats are so inclined, they can find ways to keep channels open. A range of interpretations is still possible within laws and regulations that were primarily intended to respond to domestic political pressures rather than to establish airtight controls over contacts with South Africa.

Hostile measures toward South Africa and other actions more aggressive and punitive are intended by their advocates to "quarantine" the pariah regime. To heighten South Africa's isolation is to draw attention to its repugnant social policies and to protect governments that disengage from "contamination" both in the political sense and in terms of guilt by association. These measures are, by and large, less active or threatening than either a comprehensive sanctions policy or positive support for militant opponents of apartheid. But their intent is clear, and their aggregate effect is to raise the costs of normal interstate intercourse. These messages are made up of gestures, symbols, signals. But if selectively chosen, they can be even more carefully focused and conscientiously implemented.

NONGOVERNMENTAL EFFORTS TO ISOLATE SOUTH AFRICA

Governments, individually or collectively, seek to reprimand, punish, and isolate South Africa. By contrast, private citizens, individually, as members of groups within their countries, or as members of groups that in turn belong to international nongovernmental organizations tend to mobilize to force governments to act. They also try to augment and reinforce that message of rejection, often by implementing their own versions of exclusion and boycott.

Activities against apartheid have been undertaken at all levels by a kaleidoscopic collection of movements, organizations, and groups. Some have been launched by organizations specifically created to oppose apartheid, such as the antiapartheid movements in the U.K., Netherlands, Germany, and so forth. These massive movements are skilled at organizing protest demonstrations and at lobbying legislatures and businesses. In addition, numerous other organizations only secondarily concerned with or involved in South African affairs have campaigned to ostracize South Africa on more narrow policy issues. Apartheid is the sort of high-profile emotion-laden issue that prompts strange coalitions of often unexpected bedfellows. Among those that claim to work against apartheid are groups that on the surface have occasionally been seen to support South Africa. It is not always easy to foster cooperation and coordination among the multiplicity of opponents of apartheid. Yet there have been impressive examples of international coordination among international nongovernmental organizations (NGOs) and with governments.

Most antiapartheid activity has taken place at national or subnational levels. Churches, civil rights organizations, trade unions, and student and professional organizations are persistent in their labors. They have been in the vanguard, pressing governments, businesses, and other NGOs to sever their ties with South Africa. Throughout the West they have engaged in campaigns to end bank loans to South Africa, sporting links, immigration, entertainers' tours, tourism, and student, scientific, and leadership exchanges. Almost any activity involving individuals and groups in or from South Africa has been discouraged or boycotted at one time or another. And there has been an interchangeability about these activities as their proponents dabble in affairs outside their normal concerns. Church groups pester corporations. Students hassle university boards. Civil rights groups lean on sports figures and entertainers. The World Council of Churches (WCC), the All-African Council of Churches, the Episcopal Church, the United Church of Christ, and the United Methodist Church (to mention just a few international and U.S. groups) have been active at corporate meetings, have withdrawn their monies from banks making loans to South Africa, and have recommended positions and activities to their members. Likewise, trade unions, in addition to refusing to handle shipments from or to South Africa, are involved in lobbying, sporting boycotts, and pension-fund investment decisions.

Private and group efforts to isolate South Africa have a marked international and fluid character. Coalitions have been cobbled together rapidly and sometimes in unpredictable combinations in opposition to apartheid. Many of the governmental steps to end various sorts of relations with South Africa (as discussed earlier), especially in the West, are products of intense and sometimes well-coordinated activist campaigns to galvanize governments into action. At national and international levels as well, there are umbrella organizations to orchestrate the campaigns. For instance, the UN's Center Against Apartheid monitors and encourages sanctions activities by providing activists with information, publicity, research, and organizational guidance.

Religious Exclusion

The efforts to exclude and ostracize South African counterpart organizations seem most successful in the fields of religion and sports. In 1982, for example, the World Alliance of Reformed Churches declared apartheid a theological heresy. It suspended the white Dutch Reformed Churches of South Africa from membership. Likewise, in 1984, the Lutheran World Federation expelled two small white southern African Lutheran churches for failing to unite with predominantly Black Lutheran churches in the region. Continued pressure from the WCC led the South African government to do the exclusionary work for the isolationists.

Meanwhile, Pretoria pressured all churches in South Africa to separate from the WCC and prohibited contributions to the WCC. There is increasing evidence that South Africa's whites are upset about being excluded and that they are beginning to take steps to end the racial barriers in their congregations and church organizations.

Segregation in Sports

Far more convincing has been the transformations in some, though not all, of South Africa's sporting associations.[9] No law directly forbids racially integrated sports in South Africa. Nonetheless, until recently government was able to maintain segregation by applying a variety of laws relating to liquor, separate amenities, and group areas. Because sport in South Africa revolves around clubs, which are social as much as sporting organizations, government was able to prohibit or inhibit racial mixing at clubs that lacked "international" (i.e., multiracial) status. The need to obtain permits for mixed competition also prevented players and spectators from joining together at grounds located in one group area. Beyond the national laws, provincial ordinances and local social mores made mixed sports difficult below the professional or highly visible national and provincial levels. Many of these rules had been loosened in the 1970s and 1980s, although integrators still needed the cooperation of someone in authority in order to participate in racially mixed sport.

Some say that Pretoria's desire to compete in international sport has driven it to desegregate sport in order to combat the growing isolation. Today barriers to mixing still exist. Many are the result of club decisions as well as decisions by school sporting bodies and local communities. The government may now be more willing to tolerate greater racial mixing—that is, more so on the field than in the clubhouse—but it has not interfered with decisions of clubs and local authorities that wish to maintain sports segregation.

Ironically, some Blacks in South Africa reject integration of sport even when opportunities to compete are presented. At the major universities, for example, various sporting competitions are open to all students. But Black student associations and counterpart Black student sporting clubs discourage Black students from competing in integrated teams or in what they regard as largely white competitions. Their boycotts have been nearly total. For instance, soccer in South Africa is very popular among Blacks. Yet only a handful of Blacks participated in the interuniversity soccer tournament. The boycotters argue that until all segregation is ended, they should not allow their presence to be used as an exhibit in the incomplete and meaningless reform process; sport, like most things in South Africa, has a political utility that should not be squandered.

Indeed, Pretoria's desire to use sport for political and propagandistic purposes prompted both NGOs and international governmental organizations to keep South Africa from participating internationally and to discourage athletes from other countries from visiting South Africa. For the first time in 1956, an international body, the International Table Tennis Federation, expelled the white South African body because of racial discrimination. It recognized, instead, the South African Table Tennis Board, which at the time represented Blacks but was pledged to nonracialism. In the same year, a sports pressure group was formed in South Africa to help nonracial sporting bodies gain recognition from international bodies. The government resisted their efforts, thereby further politicizing sport. It refused to issue passports to officials and athletes from nonracial federations. In 1962, an organization called the South African Non-Racial Olympic Committee (SANROC) was formed to force South Africa to end all racial barriers in sport or else to deny South African participation in the Olympics. It was successful, for South Africa was not permitted to participate in the 1964 Olympics because of its racial policies. It was also excluded from the 1968 Olympic games and expelled from the International Olympic Movement in 1972. The UN General Assembly has adopted resolutions and even a 1985 international convention on "Apartheid in Sports" calling for further isolation of South Africa, both by direct means and against third party contacts.

But these sporting exclusions snowballed. South Africa was expelled or suspended from the international governing bodies, or had its application for membership rejected, in virtually all major sports, including soccer, boxing, cycling, swimming, volleyball, weightlifting, wrestling, basketball, and track and field. Governments, international federations, and national sporting organizations have used a variety of techniques, including secondary boycotts of athletes who themselves have competed in South Africa or against South Africans. Indeed, the Olympic games and the Commonwealth games became political arenas at which states that had earlier competed officially or unofficially with South Africa or with isolated South Africans could expect to face the threat of expulsion or else the withdrawal of large coalitions of states.

The South African government has sought to get around these restrictions by declaring that it would allow the integration of their national teams and the promotion of "multinational" sporting contests in South Africa. These steps are designed to convince the world that their sports are not segregated. They also encourage "rebel" teams (made up of well-paid name players from abroad) to tour South Africa and South African teams to go abroad. In these ways they challenge the boycotters both overtly and covertly.[10] In short, Pretoria's schemes seek to encourage those inclined to shelter South Africa by providing new pretexts for doing so and confusing others ignorant of the complex realities of sport and life in South Africa.

But the issue is larger than sporting ties and racial segregation. Sport is merely the public reason for the boycott. Just as the South African government has used sport for political purposes, domestically and internationally, and has applied political and racial standards to decisions about sport, so the opponents of apartheid have countered by extracting political mileage from sporting issues.

It is clear that the changes brought about within South African sport have been instituted as a result of international pressure to change. Faced with a choice between isolation and change in sport, white South Africa has chosen to change—but as little as necessary. Although sports bodies and athletes may not be directly responsible for their country's political system, the object has been to allow the well-publicized pressure to build against the apartheid system. Any effort to open doors would relieve that pressure. And until sporting organizations in South Africa openly oppose and defy government and its apartheid policies, the foreign efforts will not be lessened. Laws that specifically prevented mixed sport have not been necessary because white sports bodies have served government's ends. For a long time, racialism was more important than the game, both for the South African authorities and to South Africa's opponents. The special position of sport in South Africa makes it particularly vulnerable to political pressure: Isolation increases the tensions and internal opposition that the government must face. Nevertheless, the issue transcends sport.

The chairman of the UN Special Committee Against Apartheid stipulated four conditions for South Africa's readmission to international sport: abolition of the homelands, a unitary educational system, equal access for every citizen to public and private sports facilities, and the end of economic apartheid.[11] Only one of those conditions deals directly with sport. And yet these demands characterize the isolationists' argument. They work not solely for total sport integration but to end apartheid in all its guises. So sport becomes instrumental to the larger political issue. In a sense, the matter is one of poetic justice, because Pretoria seeks to exploit sport for its own political ends. South Africa has been effectively excluded from around 90 percent of the world's international sporting activities. Although such action has prompted significant reform in South African sports, we cannot be sure if reform has spilled over into the political arena. Sporting isolation may add to the global opposition against apartheid, but it is not likely to be the major factor in its eventual demise. Sport, however, does play a major role by publicizing and making apartheid comprehensible to ordinary sports fans who, might not otherwise follow the politics in remote lands.

Boycotts

Much the same can be said about the entertainment and artistic boycotts of South Africa. The fundamental issue is not entertainment or art, but politics. Just as these activities have been used by the regime to break boycotts and to further apartheid's political agenda, so opponents of apartheid are prepared to use them to isolate and weaken the apartheid state. In South Africa, various unions and "cultural desks" have been set up to monitor and enforce boycotts and to help decide when such contacts further the cause of resistance. As noted in a recent statement from the National Cultural Desk (an organization affiliated with the ANC): "Apartheid legislation is still enshrined on the statute books. In this context . . . boycotts must be maintained as an integral part of peaceful and effective sanctions."

Hence, in Western states, at the UN, in the Third World, and in South Africa itself, organizations are in place to ensure that, until serious changes in apartheid are instituted, South Africa shall not have normal artistic, sporting, or entertainment relations with the world; and that only those contacts either approved by these groups or deemed to contribute to the resistance (meaning those deemed to be progressive) shall be permitted. In some respects, these various boycott guidelines present a confusing set of standards that, themselves, lead to conflict among those who seek to be artistic gatekeepers. But there is general agreement as to what is permissible and what is not.

Whereas governments seek to reprimand, punish, and isolate South Africa (or, in some cases, to appear to do so without incurring costs), private organizations try to augment that message by implementing their own versions of exclusion and rejection. But in this enterprise there sometimes seems to be a confusion of aims and policies. Government-to-government policy would seem to strike the entity most directly responsible for the regime's racist policies. Private organizations, by contrast, may or may not hit the primary target.

For example, when a boycott focuses on an exploitative South African or foreign company, that's fine. But when it damages a progressive employer, the question is whether that outcome was intended or simply the most efficient use of scarce political currency. Isolation of the Dutch Reformed Church in South Africa, for instance, tends to punish those who support government and its apartheid policies (inasmuch as most Afrikaners and members of the power structure are members of the Dutch Reformed Church). But isolation of, say, the Roman Catholic Church, of whom a large majority of communicants in South Africa are Black, the wrong segment of the population may feel abandoned.

Likewise, an effort to deny landing rights in the United States for the South African Airways (a state corporation) would tend to inconvenience and cost white South Africans more than Black ones. An embargo on textbook sales to South Africa could, however, hurt Black students if applied across the board. A severance of cricket or rugby contacts would hurt the white minority, whereas an end to soccer contacts would fall unevenly on Black sports followers. Scientific exchanges benefit whites; trade union contacts benefit Blacks. All down the line, policy trade-offs are necessary as the alleged benefits and alleged costs of each proposed measure are weighed.

The point is that private organizations with international links have the capacity to focus opprobrium and penalties more sharply than crude intergovernmental links. And yet these policy instruments are seldom employed in a discrete and selective fashion. Among committed advocates of total isolation, nothing less than a complete severance of ties makes sense. They tend to see such contacts, no matter how benign or supportive of majority concerns, in a negative light. It seems, however, that this total isolationist perspective is fading as a more mature and selective isolationist orientation begins to assert itself among apartheid's opponents.

DIRECT AID TO APARTHEID'S VICTIMS

Of course, not all opponents of apartheid are isolationists, and not all isolationists are isolationist all of the time. Their pattern has been to sever ties with official apartheid agencies and organizations that conform to apartheid dictates, but also to seek to assist and encourage those within South Africa who resist the system. Many isolationists are prepared to be engaged—but on the right side. A few examples can illustrate the nature of their activities.

In 1970, the WCC Program to Combat Racism approved a grant of $200,000 for educational and humanitarian work to the southern African liberation movements. These controversial annual grants caused extensive debate among church members and congregations about the morality of aid to liberation movements that employ force and military means. But the grants continued, totaling $2 million over the next decade. In 1971, the WCC voted overwhelmingly to withdraw its funds from corporations investing or trading in South Africa, Namibia, and the Portuguese colonies. Individual member churches were urged to press such corporations to withdraw operations from these countries.

The All-Africa Council of Churches constituting most Protestant church bodies in Africa also supports the liberation movements and is even prepared to aid them in more than humanitarian activities. The British Council of Churches in particular is active in South Africa. Its Division of International Affairs in 1979 called for economic disengagement, for British participation in an international oil boycott against South Africa, and for the British UN delegation not to veto economic sanctions. Meanwhile, the National Council of Churches of Christ in the United States has urged both government and private economic disengagement from South Africa. Through the Interfaith Center on Corporate Responsibility (supported by 17 Protestant denominations and 180 Roman Catholic orders and dioceses), church bodies coordinate their campaigns for the economic isolation of South Africa. Church groups also provide assistance for refugees and scholarship students.

Other groups support educational efforts. With scholarships, supplies, teachers' salaries, and books, they try to redress the decades of Bantu education and governmental neglect. Exiles and refugees are the beneficiaries, as are students in good standing both within and outside South Africa. Overall, private foundations, corporations, relief agencies, professional associations, universities, support organizations, and church-related groups are active on many fronts.[12] Among church organizations alone, the following types of programs have been initiated: adult and youth education, advocacy, agriculture, bursaries, business development, church and community leadership development, crisis intervention, detainee assistance, education in the United States about South Africa, emergency and refugee relief, health and nutrition, legal aid, race relations, and youth programs.

Following the escalation of violence and government repression in 1983, legal aid and support for the families of prisoners and detainees became more available. The International Defense and Aid Fund (IDAF) started in Great Britain in 1956. Now its branches in a dozen or more countries are very active as conduits for governmental and private aid to the immediate victims of apartheid. In addition, the International Commission of Jurists monitors legal proceedings, Amnesty International publicizes the plight of political prisoners, and other professional groups aid apartheid's most vulnerable victims and opponents. Reject the establishment, they say, but do not abandon the victims. The work of these organizations and many other organizations and governments is remarkably varied and often quite ingenious given the obstacles they face from Pretoria. We can barely scratch the surface of their activities.

LINKS THAT SUPPORT SOUTH AFRICA'S REGIME

There are many who contend that the very acts of continuing to trade with and maintaining diplomatic relations with South Africa are supportive of apartheid. There is no question that South Africa still deals widely and openly in commercial and financial circles, especially in the West. Moreover, the fact that South Africa maintains full diplomatic relations with less than thirty states provides Pretoria with a measure of acceptance and economic leverage to defend its system. These links are expanding again, for the first time in over three decades. In one way or another it is possible to rationalize such contacts, most of which are legal according to international law and according to the municipal law of the various states involved. In this section, however, we shall examine the extraordinary steps that strengthen apartheid and, in most cases, are intended to stabilize the status quo in South Africa.

Although not many powerful economic and political interests abroad would publicly favor apartheid, it is possible to find groups and individuals that push for continued and even expanded ties with Pretoria. A number of these groups, insofar as they oppose sanctions, disinvestment, and other efforts to ostracize South Africa, are encouraged and occasionally assisted and coordinated by the South African embassy and consulates in the countries where they are based. South Africans frequently head lobby efforts abroad. In other cases, the South African government hires public relations firms abroad to lobby on their behalf. The South African Foundation, a private organization funded largely by South African businesses and foreign firms doing business in South Africa, is active in the United States, the U.K., France, and Germany. In addition, Chambers of Commerce, service clubs, some right-of-center political associations and politicians, and joint or bilateral trade councils, most of which are private associations, are trying to stimulate contacts. Some homeland governments also retain paid lobbyists and public relations firms in the United States.

In Great Britain a range of organizations, both partisan and independent, have spoken out in support of South Africa and in opposition to various antiapartheid efforts to break with Pretoria. The Monday Club, for instance, is a coalition of ultraconservative members of the Conservative Party. Its branches throughout Britain have pressed the party rightward at the local level, in parliament, and in government. Diverse trade and business associations, supported by individual corporations, have been effective, especially when the Conservative Party has been in power, and they try to keep British interests engaged in South Africa. Chief among them are the United Kingdom–South Africa Trade Association, the South African section of the British National Export Council, the South African Society, and the Britain and South African Forum. Cultural links are stressed as well through church, language, and genealogical groups.

The Netherlands has witnessed a similar preoccupation with "blood ties" and cultural roots. Reactionary politicians and clergy have come together in the proapartheid Nederlandse Zuidafrikaanse Werkgemeenschap.[13] Less reactionary though still supportive of relations are the Zuid-Afrikaansche Stichting Moederland and the Nederlands-Zuidafrikaanse Vereniging. These groups foster continued Dutch immigration to South Africa as well as Calvinist church and university exchanges, and they oppose the international activities of Black resistance groups. Many in the business community are supportive of Dutch–South African intercourse, too. At one point, some fifty Dutch firms had subsidiaries in South Africa. Dutch firms have been implicated in efforts to break the oil embargo of South Africa; many stress trade, not investment. Antiapartheid activists, however, are working to sever these ties.

In each Western democracy, the debate rages about the policy of either isolating or engaging South Africa. Domestic forces are arrayed against one another, and there are support organizations within South Africa and in the employ of the South African government. The constellations of organizations harden as they battle for attention and favor. It is a sometimes tortuous struggle for the ear and endorsement of key policymakers.

SOUTH AFRICA'S REINTEGRATION

In testimony to the undeniable impact of the changes in South Africa's domestic socio-political and economic situation upon its international posture, it is possible to discern a countertrend toward the readmission of South Africa into the ranks of the active and welcome members of the international community.[14] Reintegration may be too strong a term. Perhaps an erosion of isolationist measures may be a more accurate description. These changes appear to be rewards of a sort for the NP government's movement toward a peaceful resolution of the Namibian dispute, the repeal of the legislation identified with apartheid, clear progress toward negotiation with the popular Black movements, and the stated intentions of government leaders to bring forth a new South Africa.

Ironically, years of careful work to isolate Pretoria might have been outdone by one event. The ceremonies marking the independence of Namibia in March 1990 were attended by South Africa's President F. W. de Klerk and dozens of representatives of other governments. In the course of thirty-six hours, de Klerk met with top officials from Western, socialist-bloc, African, and even Middle Eastern states, many of which had been systematically shunning South Africa and some of which were assisting its enemies militarily. It was a major diplomatic coup for de Klerk, in a sense undoing the diligent labor of years of behind-the-scenes lobbying. Many interpret those meetings and de Klerk's subsequent trips to Europe and the United States in 1990 as rewards for the concessions that de Klerk had made regarding Namibia and South Africa, and as a signal that the rest of the world approves of the changes he is introducing.

In the diplomatic arena, one hears less of the rhetoric associated with pariahdom. Condemnatory criticisms are generally more restrained and less frequent. Even some praise has been forthcoming. Along with that has been an increasing number of diplomatic contacts, including an exchange of diplomatic representatives with Hungary in mid-1990 and agreements to exchange trade representatives with Madagascar and Poland, open a South African trade office in Mauritius, enter into diplomatic relations with Morocco and Togo, open interests offices with Poland and the Soviet Union, and establish consular ties with Czechoslovakia and Bulgaria. Relations with Denmark and Sweden have been upgraded as well. Missions have been opened in six unnamed African cities and will be opened in three more cities in 1991.

Top-level political visits have been frequent, particularly of South African officials abroad. President de Klerk visited 16 states in 1990, including the United States, Britain, France, Germany, Italy, Morocco, Madagascar, Senegal, and the Ivory Coast, to meet their heads of government and state. Some ministers of state were even more active. As of yet no foreign head of state or government has visited South Africa, but a few top officials from abroad have arrived. Considering that the ANC is still advocating South Africa's diplomatic isolation, these have been significant breakthroughs.

Although there has been no formal reentry of South Africa into intergovernmental organizations, that pattern, too, may soon be altered. Business organizations in South Africa and elsewhere have urged that South Africa be afforded observer status in the Southern African Development Coordination Conference (SADCC) and the Preferential Trade Area of Eastern and Southern Africa.

Steps to ease sanctions are in progress, including the European Community's decision to lift the ban on new investments in South Africa (as of December 15, 1990) and promises to ease other measures as soon as the government introduces legislation to abolish particular apartheid laws. In other cases, foreign governments have said that they would end sanctions when the proposed laws are enacted. Only the OAU continues to maintain a hard line. They think that sanctions should be kept in place until full agreement is reached in South Africa on the process for drawing up a new constitution and for the transition to a democratic order, including the holding of elections.

Various bodies are reviewing their positions on cultural and sports boycotts, too. Tentative steps have been taken toward South Africa's readmission into various international bodies. An investigatory committee for the International Olympic Committee visited South Africa in March

1991 and outlined steps toward South Africa's reentry into that organization. The British and Australian governments have called for a
relaxation of sports bans under the Commonwealth's Gleneagles Agreement of 1977, which discouraged all sporting ties with South Africa.
Cultural exchanges are more common. South African artists based abroad
are returning to perform in their home country. Foreign entertainers in
selected cases have been approved by the "cultural desks." There is a
fresh wind of expectation blowing across the country.

The basic question that all groups that formerly ostracized South
Africa must now answer is one of timing—when is the most effective
time to reopen links with South Africa and under what terms or
conditions? Isolation as a policy has become yesterday's issue, but
reintegration may be premature, especially if the outside world still
possesses leverage. The world community looks to events and to popular
Black leaders in South Africa for guidance on any policy shifts.

CONCLUSION

Generally, the supporters of apartheid have been silenced in top
policy councils in the West. There may be leaders sympathetic to the
white minority and others nostalgic for the "orderly" and stable time
of white rule and Black obedience, but few today would openly endorse
apartheid. Accordingly, those who favor policies of disengagement and
isolation, and those favoring the opposite, engagement and intercourse,
both push their policy preferences under the guise of wanting to do
something about apartheid.

Advocates of disengagement point to the uniqueness of South Africa's
racial order. If nothing is done, if pressure is not raised, they contend,
little of a progressive nature will be accomplished because the government
there will not be motivated to take positive steps to end apartheid. A
do-nothing policy is seen by such advocates as contributing to an
eventual and violent conflict, with those in power wielding the upper
hand. As before, a continuance of ties would reinforce those already
favored by the system. In the past, appeals to reason and extensive
foreign involvement with the regime in Pretoria did not prompt progressive change. Only positive steps showing that business as usual
cannot go on indefinitely seem to grab Pretoria's attention. Authority
unchallenged seldom questions itself. And rarely do authoritarians vol-
untarily surrender power or initiate reform. The least violent and most
poignant message of disapproval is to sever ties with the regime. In
other words, there is a moral imperative to act before full-scale civil
war breaks out.

Then there is the economic consideration that, contrary to popular wisdom, capitalist growth and apartheid are compatible. In the past, many assumed that the necessity for a skilled and committed work force would compel apartheid ideologues to come to terms with the economic growth powered by foreign trade, investment, and technology. But the fact is that South Africa has never had a totally free and mobile labor force responsive to market imperatives. Although inefficiency is built into the system, the inequities are so great and the profits so attractive that capital finds a way to live with apartheid laws and mores. That being more or less the case, further investment does not undermine apartheid; it adapts to apartheid. Thus disengagement is required to alter the unequal power relationships radically.

In addition, as long as the West continues to deal with Pretoria in ways that it has in the past, Western foreign policy will not be credibly antiapartheid. At present, those who trade with and invest in South Africa are "identified" with Pretoria and thus "implicated." They are "partners" or "accomplices" of apartheid. Spoken criticisms are not enough, because in South Africa they are not taken seriously. The regime reads them correctly—as obligatory lip service intended to deflect critics at home while simultaneously maintaining advantageous or profitable relations. Indeed, South Africa uses evidence of open contact for its political purposes.

For many, disengagement is a matter of principle and a symbol of where they stand. For others, economic disengagement does more than embarrass the South African regime and make a moral statement of rejection—it weakens apartheid. It increases the costs of maintaining the system.

The counterargument of those opposed to disengagement seems to turn on the very same question: Just what impact would rapid economic growth fueled from outside have on political relations in South Africa? Greater foreign investment tends to be in capital intensive industry. The migratory labor system, based largely on cheap, unskilled or semiskilled short-term workers, cannot efficiently serve a sophisticated and technologically advanced economy. Growing mechanization requires a new labor policy, which in turn demands new educational programs and new housing patterns for a stable work force. A homelands scheme that contributes to an insecure and distant work force cannot be economically rational. Job reservation (the practice of reserving certain jobs for certain race groups), the color bar, and the refusal to allow workers of color to supervise white workers have been shown to be uneconomical and outdated. These old-style apartheid policies have been grudgingly abandoned by the regime, though with considerable white opposition.

Seen from this perspective, economic growth would seem to undermine apartheid. What is more, a booming economy and expanding production depend on a growing consumer market. In South Africa, this means the Black market, since the white market is virtually saturated. African income will have to be increased, thus possibly leading to conflict when material expectations are frustrated or when the economy hits a stagnant patch. According to this view, industrialization cannot help but lead to democratization and Black empowerment. There is some evidence to suggest that, if the white power structure senses that control is slipping away, it would not hesitate to make economic sacrifices to ensure political power. There is also some evidence to the contrary.

Nonetheless, supporters of engagement insist that although economic development may strengthen white supremacy in the short run, it undermines the racist order in the long run. Given the limited white manpower, growth requires that skilled positions eventually be filled by Blacks. In short, the economy becomes to some extent dependent on the Black population. These circumstances provide Blacks with a source of potential power, as attested by the rise of the Black trade union movement in the last decade. Whether this evolving situation works to weaken or strengthen minority power is unclear. Modern defenders of the South African regime are determined to coopt the growing Black bourgeoisie—to give them a stake in the system—and thereby enlist them to defend a steadily reforming status quo. In other words, they hope to trade them material benefits for political power.

But this objective confuses economic and political agendas. Under P. W. Botha, co-optation was the strategy. Selected Black "representatives"— those operating within the official structures in the homelands, municipalities, and local councils—were identified and courted. This strategy was predicated on "securocratic" thinking, however: security or stability first; then consult with malleable Blacks on government's terms. Weaken the Black opposition; then dictate to them what you are prepared to concede by way of political representation, rather than which of their demands you are prepared to accept. It is not negotiation in any genuine sense—it is consultation with "acceptable" Black voices. But what is acceptable to the minority government, it turns out, is not acceptable to the Black masses. This approach failed badly to make progress toward a resolution of differences and was abandoned by the new NP leadership.

Under de Klerk, the new thinking in government requires that a climate be established leading to negotiations with the authentic, not the coopted, leaders of the Black masses. The effort to identify pliable Blacks is still on the back burner, but it is likely to be used if the option focusing on dealing with the ANC and its allies falters. Interestingly, the ANC has expressed a desire to include some "system" Blacks (e.g., selected homeland leaders and Coloured representatives) in serious constitutional talks. The ANC is determined, in its way, to include the Black bourgeoisie as well as sympathetic white liberals and radicals, so that together they can confront the white power structure.

There is an additional dimension to the argument of those who favor keeping their ties with South Africa. Even if we find apartheid morally abhorrent, they ask, are we personally or is our country responsible for the tragic state of affairs in South Africa? There are dozens of other inhumane political systems that we seem less concerned about. Rather than launch another crusade to change another country, we should read more modestly our capacities for affecting life positively elsewhere.[15] If we realize that it is not our duty to keep the peace around the globe, we might also understand that we better serve our interests by not overextending ourselves and by keeping avenues of contact open. The matter is one of quasi-isolationist rejection of those activists who seek to isolate South Africa.

To what extent do white supremacists in South Africa, or simply white South African nationalists, become more xenophobic and more resistant to change because they are under pressure from foreigners? Would such pressure merely intensify their efforts to become self-reliant and to resist serious change? Indeed, could South Africa actually achieve self-sufficiency in the context of the global political economy of the late twentieth century?

And would measures that reduce or end Western contacts with South Africa actually weaken the West's ability to influence Pretoria? In the short run, measures to isolate South Africa do hamper dialogue with Pretoria and the ability to open South African minds. How many times have visitors to South Africa been cornered by South African intellectuals and artists who rail against boycotts by U.S. or British book publishers, artists, athletes, and academics? "How can we change the views of our close-minded countrymen if we cannot show them what the rest of the world thinks of them and how contemporary art and ideas are evolving? Don't leave us hanging out there, alone!" Isolation not only punished those South Africans with a greater international vision and subjected them to accusations of treason and disloyalty; it also reinforced the narrow-minded sorts who seemed to prefer to go it alone or to be belligerent in a hostile world. How can the South African government be brought to see the folly of its apartheid ways if the points of contact and possible enlightenment are systematically severed? South Africa, the engagers argue, might be in danger of drifting into sterile isolation. Persuasion cannot be exercised in a vacuum; conflicting views cannot be reconciled in absentia. They would contend that, although disengagement and isolation may cleanse the soul, it doesn't necessarily end apartheid. It is a form of washing one's hands of an evil for which the West is partially responsible. Isolation, therefore, dooms South Africa's Black population to inertia or, worse, to a violent and lonely struggle toward a revolution that may or may not succeed.

It is a perverse logic which insists that in order to have an impact on another society, one must renounce the very instruments of policy or points of contact (and hence leverage) that one possesses. Nevertheless, by choosing not to change policy—that is, by staying in and interacting with South Africa—an actor in effect acquiesces to a morally objectionable status quo. The simple fact is that the United States' instruments of foreign policy are not precise or selective enough to hurt those it wishes to hurt or to reward or assist those it wishes to favor. This is the dilemma inherent in dealing with South Africa. It would seem that if the real advocates of engagement argue for the retention of links because links are a form of leverage, then they are obliged to demonstrate clearly that they are using or are prepared to use the levers of power to expedite change. Yet most foreign advocates of continued links did little in the past to try to change South Africa. Their appeals against ending ties seem more akin to ex post facto rationalizations for a do-nothing policy that they have gained from and been comfortable with in the past. Doing nothing, business as usual, however, is not a viable option for ending apartheid in the 1990s.

SIX

□ □ □

Defending Apartheid, Projecting Power, and the Arms Embargoes

A natural consequence of the attempts to ostracize South Africa and the global effort to bring an end to apartheid is the feeling on the part of South Africa's ruling elite and the citizens who support it that the world is ganging up on them. They are partly right: The overwhelming majority of governments in the world *are* critical of apartheid and keen on forcing South Africa to change. This perspective was summed up as a case of "total onslaught," a term, as noted earlier, that came into vogue in security and government circles in the late 1970s. Pretoria downplayed the total onslaught line in the middle and late 1980s, preferring instead to define the threat as "multidimensional." But its perspective remained essentially the same. Hence policymaking was preoccupied with the security and the military aspects of security until P. W. Botha's demise in 1989.

There had been a conviction throughout this period that South Africa was being unfairly singled out, that Marxist opponents were behind the onslaught, that it was inspired from abroad and coordinated by the communist powers, and, accordingly, that a total onslaught demanded a "total national strategy" to counter it. The onslaught was believed to be not just military but also political, diplomatic, religious, psychological, cultural, economic, and social. According to the government's *White Paper on Defence and Armaments Supply, 1982*:

> The ultimate aim of the Soviet Union and its allies is to overthrow the present body politic in the RSA [Republic of South Africa] and to replace

it with a Marxist-orientated form of government to further the objectives of the USSR, therefore all possible methods and means are used to attain this objective. This includes instigating social and labour unrest, civilian resistance, terrorist attacks against the infrastructure of the RSA and the intimidation of Black leaders and members of the Security Forces. This onslaught is supported by a worldwide propaganda campaign and the involvement of various front organizations and leaders.[1]

Hence the security establishment regarded the efforts to isolate South Africa and undermine apartheid as elements of the total onslaught. Insofar as the West cooperates in these designs, this cooperation is being used, in the words of P. W. Botha, "in an attempt to pay a ransom to the bear whose hunger must be satisfied."[2]

Botha and his securocrats were wrong, however, in assuming that this was an orchestrated and well-planned scheme to undermine South African society, and that it involved most segments of the international community and was directed from Moscow or any other podium of power. As we have seen in earlier chapters, the international community simply does not operate that way. Dozens, indeed hundreds, of campaigns and endeavors—some cooperative to one degree or another, some individualistic and ad hoc, some imitative and others highly idiosyncratic, some others resistant to the isolationist and hostile mood—make up the sum total of policy that Botha's propagandists chose to label the "total onslaught."

But the question of whether their perceptions of world politics were correct mattered little within South Africa itself. Local opponents of the regime were under fire, accused of being in league with the Soviet Union or of being used by Moscow, or else of inadvertently assisting the forces of chaos and revolution. Total onslaught provided an excuse for consolidating power, silencing critics, and punishing opponents. In domestic South African policy and in foreign policy, the SADF became the preferred instrument for implementing the "total national strategy."

Virtually every facet of public life and many facets of private life were fit topics for government policy. Because the onslaught directed at South Africa was considered to be communist-inspired, South Africa regarded itself as the keystone in the defense of "the whole free Western world." Pretoria has included itself in the "free world." The contest is more than political—it is ideological and even religious. "It is a struggle," said Prime Minister Botha, "between the powers of chaos, Marxism and destruction on the one hand and the powers of order, Christian civilization and the upliftment of people on the other."[3]

Pretoria misreads the West on this issue. Western governments, such as those of Ronald Reagan and George Bush in the United States, the

Conservatives in Great Britain, Helmut Kohl in Germany, and even various French governments, are impressed by the strategic and psychological dangers posed by a global communist challenge. They have retained that concern even after the decline of socialism in eastern Europe. But they also realize not only that the Soviet threat is marginal in southern Africa, but also that apartheid is morally unacceptable and that a too-close identification with an aggressive racist apartheid would be costly in terms of their policies in the Third World. Along with Pretoria, they may be desirous of keeping the communists out of southern Africa; but they disagree—especially now, in the 1990s—with Pretoria's strategy for doing so. The West realizes that the instability in the region grew directly out of South Africa's domestic racism and Pretoria's desire to defend apartheid by carrying the struggle to its enemies beyond its borders.

Crucial to the maintenance of the South African regime was the need to devise a comprehensive counterrevolutionary strategy. Under P. W. Botha and his minister of defense, General Magnus Malan, a total national strategy was fashioned that deepened the involvement of the defense establishment in diverse aspects of civilian life and emphasized the security and defense posture of South Africa. The securocrats were unwilling or unable, however, to address the underlying causes of South Africa's political bankruptcy, economic limitations, and discredited pattern of race relations embodied in the rubric of apartheid.

In this chapter we shall discuss several of the issues that emerge where state security and foreign affairs collide. Among them are arms embargoes, nuclear technology and weapons, South Africa's efforts to destabilize neighboring states in the region, and the strategic philosophy of total onslaught. These issues represent the confluence of South Africa's desire to defend and maintain the apartheid state or, as old-line Nationalists would say, "the South African way," and the world's desire to end apartheid by reducing South Africa's ability to function militarily.

WEAPONS EMBARGOES

Chief among Pretoria's anxieties has been the perceived need to maintain efficient and modern armed forces to defend the regime. Yet one of the first manifestations of international opposition was the effort to mount an international arms embargo against South Africa. The arms embargo seems to many governments the most obvious and direct first policy step to weaken the ability of Pretoria to maintain its system, largely because that system rests upon the calculated use of force and violence to terrorize its opponents and enemies, and because the embargo directly targets those in positions of power in South Africa.

Since 1963, no fewer than four Security Council resolutions have been passed prohibiting the export of armaments and military and nuclear technology to South Africa as well as the import of armaments made in South Africa. Despite these embargoes, some trade in armaments continues. The very Western governments that agreed in the UN to enforce the arms restrictions have found ways to evade sanctions. Such evasions have enabled South Africa to build an advanced military-industrial complex that in effect makes South Africa self-sufficient in small weapons, ammunition, military vehicles, and the sorts of low-level military materiel most useful in combating guerrilla wars and civil unrest.

The pattern of embargo developed as follows. Security Council Resolution 181 of August 7, 1963, called for a *voluntary* cessation of all sales of armaments and other military equipment. And on December 4, 1963, Resolution 182 covered equipment and materials that would facilitate arms production in South Africa. More important, these two resolutions were made *mandatory* by Resolution 418 of November 4, 1977, which also embargoed cooperation with South Africa in the development and manufacture of nuclear weapons. The latest Security Council resolution on arms (Resolution 558 of December 13, 1984) requests that all states refrain from importing arms, ammunition, and military vehicles produced in South Africa.

It is important to see the arms embargo as a selected form of economic sanctions. But an arms embargo is more focused than comprehensive economic sanctions inasmuch as it directly affects the government and the regime and, when it works, weakens their ability to project power against neighbors and against their own subjugated peoples. But the arms embargo must also be seen as a compromise. The various arms resolutions were approved after heightened demands for mandatory economic sanctions. When the Western powers finally agreed under pressure to arms resolutions, they did so as an alternative to mandatory economic sanctions.

So far, the various arms embargoes have had marginal success in reducing South Africa's military capabilities. South Africa has been able to import certain types of military technology in spite of UN embargoes. The South African armaments industry, centered around the parastatal corporation, **Armscor** (the Armaments Corporation of South Africa), owes its development to foreign inputs at various levels. It has resourcefully managed to stay steps ahead of enforcement mechanisms, such as they are. Before the first embargo, South Africa had arranged to import complete weapons systems and to place orders that were honored long after the resolution was passed. After weapons sales were embargoed, South Africa sought technologies to enable it to produce materiel domestically. With the switch from arms purchases to arms production, components and component technologies were acquired from a great variety of sources abroad. The mandatory embargo of 1977 ended the acquisition of production licenses for foreign-designed weapons systems. But without licenses, Armscor subsidiaries could still manufacture a modified weapon without the need to pay fees or royalties. The search is still on for high-technology items and for technological processes from foreign industries. Their transfer is easier to hide than weapons transfers and harder to define as strictly military goods and applications.

Loopholes in the embargo resolutions and in various foreign statutes designed to implement the embargoes have enabled governments and corporations to evade the spirit of the resolutions. Bear in mind that Pretoria is determined to acquire the capacity to produce armaments— at whatever cost. And given the diversity and decentralization of arms production in the world, black, grey, and open markets flourish at all technological levels, in order to provide both legitimate defense and support for repressive despots. The following is a list of the methods by which South Africa and its foreign industrial partners "disimplemented" the embargoes (to use Signe Landgren's term):[4]

1. *Licensed Production.* Most licenses were acquired just before the first voluntary arms embargo. All subsequent production agreements were concluded before the mandatory embargo of 1977. Once signed, contracts are hardly ever broken or canceled.
2. *Multinational Corporations and Banks.* Banks have been a critical source of finance for the military sector of the economy and thus a major source of military technology, especially in the electronics and other dual-purpose industries. When **multinational corporations** (MNCs) leave South Africa, their technology remains and is usually sold to local firms. According to South African law, subsidiaries of MNCs in South Africa are compelled to sell to Armscor and the SADF, and may not comply with instructions from their home offices on these matters without prior permission from the South African government.
3. *Direct Investment in Overseas Strategic Industries.* In effect, technological know-how cannot be denied the major owner of a company, even if that owner is South African. South African firms own significant blocks of shares in Siemens (Germany), Plessy Electronics (U.K.), and Marconi (U.K.), and in that way they directly circumvent arms trade sanctions.
4. *Cover Companies.* An elaborate network of paper or dummy companies has been constructed to protect trade links in the

event of general sanctions. These companies effectively mask the origins and destinations of strategically critical imports.

5. *Dual-Purpose or Grey-Area Equipment.* The absence of a universally agreed-upon definition of "weapons" permits sales of materiel that can be modified for military uses.

6. *Supply Operations.* The supply of spare parts and of support and maintenance equipment for existing projects continues under contract.

7. *Foreign Experts.* Foreign skills are used, as are experts from abroad, to train and educate South Africans.

8. *Renting and Leasing.* Special technologies, especially computer equipment, are leased and rented.

9. *Evasion of End-Use Agreements.* Third-country deliveries are used to violate end-use agreements drafted to prevent re-exportation to South Africa.

10. *Smuggling of Arms, Blueprints and Components.* The tighter the embargo, the more extensively South Africa will use secret and private suppliers, black market shipments, and other illegal ruses. Some of these deals are highly complex, use a number of agents, and are very difficult to trace. Few governments are organized to prevent or uncover these arrangements.

Nonetheless, efforts to evade arms sanctions have raised the costs to South Africa immensely. The political spinoffs of heightened awareness and the political steps taken to follow up on the arms embargo have forced South Africa to divert energies from other important enterprises. Moreover, the fact that military collaboration with South Africa has been criminalized has had an impact on Pretoria's ability to dictate policy in the region and in South Africa.

NUCLEAR TECHNOLOGY AND NUCLEAR WEAPONS

For almost fifteen years, South Africa's weapons capability as well as its intentions regarding nuclear weapons have been hidden from public view.[5] In August 1977, the Soviet Union alerted the United States, the U.K., France, and West Germany to what appeared to be the construction of a nuclear test site in the Kalahari Desert of the Northern Cape. At that time such notice was a rare exercise in East-West cooperation. High-resolution satellite photographs revealed a cluster of buildings around a prominent tower. A hole in the ground nearby added to the mystery. Unable to link this configuration with possible nonnuclear activities, some U.S. officials attributed it to preparations for a nuclear test.

At the time, the Carter administration was anxious about the proliferation of nuclear weapons. South Africa is not among the signatories
to the 1968 Non-Proliferation Treaty (NPT), in which more than 130
signatories promise neither to acquire nuclear weapons nor to help other
nations to do so. The United States was particularly concerned because
it had, under contract, supplied South Africa with enriched uranium.
France, too, had helped South Africa build nuclear power stations. The
United States and France joined Britain and West Germany in their
efforts to secure a firm denial from Pretoria. Although South African
officials denied that the Kalahari site had anything to do with nuclear
weapons, their statements were ambiguous, inconsistent, and uncon-
vincing. Analysts and intelligence experts can only hypothesize about
South Africa's intentions, but it would seem that South Africa was
preparing the site for testing and that problems at its top-secret Valindaba
enrichment facility forced it to call off the test and dismantle the site.
U.S. efforts to get South Africa to sign the NPT broke down in late
1978 because South Africa was not willing to open Valindaba to
International Atomic Energy Agency inspection as required by the NPT.

The issue did not rest. In September 1979, a U.S. intelligence satellite,
the Vela, recorded a double flash of light—an event unique to nuclear
explosions—as it passed over a remote expanse of ocean between South
Africa and Antarctica. Again, the analysts worried. There were no other
plausible explanations, and yet corroborating evidence was either missing
or subject to conflicting interpretation. The defense, scientific, and intelligence communities were of the view that a nuclear explosion had
occurred. But the case for a nuclear explosion remained unproven
according to official, political Washington. Even if it could be demonstrated
that a nuclear device had been exploded, just who had detonated it
remained unclear. Some blamed India, others Israel, still others South
Africa. Even more likely was a joint Israeli–South African test. If the
Vela incident was a South African test (as many believe), it appears to
have followed logically out of the Kalahari contretemps.[6]

Whatever the reality, the perception remains among experts that South
Africa does possess a nuclear capability. Yet, militarily speaking, South
Africa seems to have no plausible targets or strategic purposes for its
nuclear weapons. Hence South Africa's military need for nuclear weapons
is questionable.

But there are other serious advantages that strengthen Pretoria's hand.
Commercial considerations relating to the export and enrichment of
uranium are potentially important. So are the psychological drive to be
recognized as a regional superpower and the domestic political arguments
that the NP can use to bolster white morale. It was hoped that the
recognition of South Africa as a nuclear weapons state, the first in the

region, would provide entry into various international forums and establish bargaining leverage in wider international negotiations. Nor have these considerations prevented Pretoria from continuing to deal in nuclear fuel and equipment with its Western trading partners. South Africa's experience after the Kalahari and Vela incidents is that the Western world seems to take South Africa more seriously when nuclear weapons are involved. A nuclear threat does serve diplomatic purposes.

Pretoria conducted negotiations with the IAEA in 1985 and 1986 about the application of international safeguards to specific facilities—but to no avail. Off and on, in 1984, 1987, and again in 1990, South Africa hinted that it was prepared to explore the possibilities of signing the NPT. But talks at various levels broke down. At present, South Africa states that it will observe NPT and Nuclear Suppliers Group rules, but it refuses to sign the NPT. The chief reason is that such a signing would commit South Africa to allow its nuclear facilities, including the enrichment facility at Valindaba, to be subjected to inspection by the IAEA. Pretoria not only sees this as a matter of strategic secrecy; it also maintains that IAEA inspections might compromise certain commercial secrets of South Africa's presumably distinctive enrichment process.

ASSESSING THE IMPACT OF THE EMBARGOES

Arms embargoes and nuclear policy are discussed in some detail here because they demonstrate how international efforts to deal with apartheid and South Africa's racist regime can have unexpected and unintended results. They also show how thorny it is to assess the overall effect of a policy—how hard it is to weigh the successes and failures of a policy even after it has been in place for some time and, indeed, how difficult it is to determine the criteria for success and failure in policy evaluation.

Take the matter of arms embargoes. Few would be so naive as to think that the embargoes would lead directly to the fall of the NP government or to an expeditious end to apartheid. But if the embargoes are seen as just one among many ways to pressure Pretoria, contributing to the eventual collapse of the apartheid regime, then the results are subject to varying interpretations. Some of the countries that supported the arms embargo were totally committed to destroying apartheid and tried to limit the ability of South Africa's security establishment to repress its population and to threaten neighboring states. Their statement of opposition was fairly clear. Others were expressing an ambiguous opposition to apartheid. Together they were less than successful in ending South Africa's repressive capabilities. What had greater success was the reduction of South Africa's ability to project power abroad. Indeed, a case can be made that South Africa's air losses in Angola and its inability to replace combat aircraft lost there, and hence its need to seek a negotiated settlement on Angola and Namibia, are direct products of the cumulative military isolation brought on by the embargoes.

Some claim that the most apparent effect of the arms embargoes has been counterproductive, for it has stimulated the buildup of a domestic South African arms industry. As early as 1960, in anticipation of the eventual cutoff from traditional weapons suppliers (especially Great Britain), South Africa attempted to strengthen its already active arms industry, which had been vigorously developed during World War II. Before 1963, South Africa spent about 70 percent of its arms procurement budget overseas. Twenty years later, nearly 100 percent was being spent within South Africa on locally produced materiel. With this changeover came a greater sense of self-reliance and confidence. Self-sufficiency of a sort has been achieved, but self-sufficiency is a relative concept inasmuch as expectations may have to be lowered in order to achieve it. Although gold-generated revenues helped in large part to finance the growing weapons budgets, the embargoes inflated costs and made the acquisition of certain weapons systems difficult.

There have been marked improvements in some technologies, deterioration over time in others. South Africa is still vulnerable in key sectors of armaments, especially high-performance aircraft, helicopters, electronics and computers, and naval vessels. By contrast, South Africa has achieved high levels of self-sufficiency in ammunition, low-technology equipment, military vehicles, small and medium weaponry, light aircraft, and communications equipment. The great deal of research done in the weaponry and defense industries has spurred further exploration in related fields such as energy, materials, metals, automotive and commercial vehicles, and chemicals. Significant advances have resulted.

Overall, the general level of consciousness about security has been raised, among South Africa's defense planners, the industrial elite, and the general population. Various statutes have resulted, designed to facilitate self-sufficiency and to offset the impact of South Africa's growing military isolation. As security planners see it, South Africa's defense capabilities are lowered if any major sector of the economy is made vulnerable. The local content program (which establishes minimum proportions of a product that must be manufactured locally) in automobiles, government's encouragement of a local diesel industry, the National Key Points Act of 1980 (which protects vital infrastructural and industrial installations), the Atomic Energy Act as amended, and the National Supplies Procurement Act, among other pieces of legislation, require that private firms, including foreign-owned firms, maintain secrecy about their production levels, sources of supply, trading partners, and so forth.

At first glance, the international arms embargo of South Africa seems to have fostered a stronger, more determined white minority regime with a greater capacity to maintain itself in power. But that is a superficial appraisal. Let's look at the other side. What has the arms embargo achieved that its advocates would regard as benefits or successes? First, the embargoes have substantially raised the costs of procurement and supply. Locally manufactured products with their high R&D costs and smaller production runs are not always cheaper than products that can be purchased abroad. The higher up the technological ladder a weapons system is, the greater the differential in price for units produced with small production runs. Regardless of whether South Africa needs to purchase through agents who are prepared to violate embargoes, or to develop its own weapons systems and manufacture locally, it will have to pay more to acquire the materiel to defend itself and maintain order. Reduced supplies legitimately available to South Africa force up prices. And those operating on the fringes of legality and beyond charge handsomely for their services.

Second, regardless of cost, some weapons systems and production technologies are no longer available to South Africa. The country is neither free to enter the market in all products nor able to substitute its own indigenously developed products in all cases. For example, high-performance combat jet aircraft are no longer available to the South African Air Force. The indigenously designed Cheetah, a 50 percent reconstruction of the now 26-year-old Mirage-3, is hardly state of the art. It draws heavily on Israeli and French know-how. Moreover, it does not add to the air force inventory. It merely requires that a number of the existing fleet be modified. More than half of South Africa's Mirages are already grounded because of a shortage of spare parts and equipment. However, there is evidence that Argentina sold Mirage-3 fighter-bombers to South Africa around 1988, in violation of the UN embargo. The B-12 Canberra bomber aircraft delivered from Britain in 1962 and 1965 have been extensively refitted. The British-supplied Buccaneer naval bomber fleet, in service since 1965, was laid to rest in 1985. The Avro Shackleton long-range maritime patrol aircraft, supplied back in 1954, were phased out in 1984. None of these models have been replaced, thanks to the international embargoes. Angola's enhanced surface-to-air missiles, deployed in southern Angola, forced Pretoria to reassess its willingness to risk losing more of its inadequate and aging aircraft. The embargo did indeed take a toll.

South Africa's inability to acquire foreign-made large ships has forced the navy to change its combat function, from a blue-water navy responsible for the security of the Cape route to a coastal defense navy concerned chiefly with defending against insurgencies and infiltration. Foreign technology has been denied to the South African shipbuilding companies. As a result, local construction of frigates, corvettes, and submarines has not materialized. The last naval ships were delivered to South Africa in 1972 and 1973, and these were minor vessels. Thus we have seen just a few examples of the difficulties South Africa faces in maintaining modern armed forces. Denial of weapons and technology systems, increased costs, and delayed deliveries sometimes add up to second-rate equipment, especially when South Africa is confronted by the more modern weaponry supplied by the Soviet Union to its African allies.

Third, and this is to be expected, South Africa's determination to be militarily ready means that it must divert resources from other pressing policy areas. Research on defense-related projects is a drain on the limited educated manpower. Funds spent on defense are funds denied to housing, education, health care, and water resources—to name just a few examples. So, while South African whites may be prepared to defend the regime, dissatisfaction continues to grow out of increased deprivation inside the country. The security problems faced by the regime are in turn compounded.

Despite the growth of Armscor and an indigenous military-industrial complex, the embargoes have also prevented the open sale and export of South African–produced military equipment. As a result, larger production runs, designed to reduce per-unit costs, have not been common enough to offset the greater drain due to arms embargoes.

Clearly, however, the most profound ramifications of the embargoes occur in the realm of international politics. Arms embargoes help to influence Western governments to persist in their efforts to isolate Pretoria. And the legal frameworks put into place in each country to implement and enforce the embargoes, though admittedly less than complete, serve to criminalize collaboration with South Africa. Had arms embargoes not been enacted, the West would likely have sustained the status quo, without directly challenging the regime. Thus, the arms embargoes not only politicize and raise levels of awareness among Western elites about South Africa but also energize opposition against South Africa. Such an awareness leads otherwise apolitical elements in the West to appreciate the extent to which their trade and contact with Pretoria are used for control and repression, and to consider how they, as citizens of Western countries, might contribute to positive change in South Africa.

The arms embargoes, as with sanctions in general, provide lessons for future policymakers in similar circumstances. From these arms embargoes they can learn that a resourceful country, such as South Africa, can readily find ways to continue military imports and local manufacturing because (1) there has been no commonly agreed-upon list of the types of goods considered "military" and of the technologies with military applications, (2) there is no central monitoring agency to supervise, investigate, and prosecute cases of evasion, and (3) there are insufficient resources committed to enforcement.

At present, each country is expected to undertake all three activities within its jurisdiction. As a result, commitment to the embargoes is uneven—just as the Western governments may have wanted it. The United States is relatively conscientious in its enforcement, although its list of embargoed goods is narrow. By contrast, Israel, France, and Italy are relatively lenient in their military intercourse with South Africa; in the late 1980s, however, there was a considerable tightening of the embargoes in France and Italy. The UN embargo depends for its implementation on national governments that do not have a shared commitment to a common end. It is unlikely that governments and leaders will learn from this embargo process and correct for its inadequacies, now that a reform and negotiation process has begun in South Africa. But future embargoes against other states may benefit from what can be learned from the hit-or-miss approach to the South African arms embargoes.

DESTABILIZATION: WHY?

Beginning in the 1960s with South Africa's clandestine military assistance to the breakaway settler government in Rhodesia and to Portugal in the conduct of its colonial wars in Angola and Mozambique, and then on a more direct and larger scale with the SADF's invasion of Angola in 1975 and 1976, South Africa has been extensively involved in military operations in the region, sometimes far beyond its borders. Although many of these operations had immediate military and political purposes, they also had the effect (and the intention) of destabilizing the social, economic, and political life in neighboring states and of terrorizing the people.[7] These operations were not, as some in Pretoria contend, merely a number of ad hoc responses to perceived threats and stimuli. Rather, they exhibit a pattern of intimidation and coercion aimed at governments and peoples already critical of apartheid and vulnerable to military incursion.

It is pointless to detail the various and numerous operations, charges, and denials. Suffice to say that the list is long and damning. What is more, the revelations about police and military hit squads, cross-border strikes, and incursions—many made public after the fact in the wake of F. W. de Klerk's efforts to free his government from the undue influence of the securocrats close to Botha—confirm the speculation and accusation.

In volume, direct destabilizing activities probably reached a peak in late 1982 and early 1983 and then again from 1985 to 1987. But they have not been entirely ended, as is especially the case with proxy operations and clandestine "dirty tricks."

The aggressive and often preemptive defense of South Africa and South Africa's presence in Namibia, as well as the schemes to destroy the ANC and SWAPO personnel, bases, and offices in Angola, Zimbabwe, Zambia, Lesotho, Swaziland, Mozambique, and Botswana, are the most obvious displays of violence. But these have been compounded by border incursions, military overflights, short- and long-term territorial occupations (especially in Angola), many of which seemed to have little to do with sanctuaries for the ANC or SWAPO, assassination attempts, parcel bombs, hit squads, sabotage, intelligence operations, and "dirty tricks," as well as by extensive encouragement, training, aid, assistance, and sanctuary to dissidents, parties, and bandit groups aimed against neighboring governments. All of these factors add up to a systematic South African objective to do widespread destruction in the region. The SADF's work through proxies still goes on. Although South Africa has officially ended its assistance to UNITA in Angola, it (or official state agencies) may still have links with Renamo despite treaty obligations since 1984 to end those ties.[8]

Pretoria's objective had been not only to incapacitate its political enemies based abroad but also to bring governments in the region to the desperate realization that if they aid South Africa's enemies in any way, they will be vulnerable and will pay dearly for their cheek. Resort to violent actions has demonstrated how Pretoria's diplomatic and military policies were coordinated and complementary and, on occasion, how they were not. Overall, they were parts of a single policy, what has been called a dual strategy toward governments nearby. At times the dominant thrust was coercive. Policy by coercion and proxy is a measure of a pariah state caught in a deteriorating regional political balance. Facing the rising tide of Black nationalism after the independence of Angola, Mozambique, and Zimbabwe, and the increasing proximity of SWAPO and ANC bases, Pretoria's leaders sought to seize the initiative and to demonstrate their determination both to oppose the inevitable independence of Namibia passively and to resist the demands for a majority government in South Africa itself. Indeed, in Pretoria there had been considerable hope that governments could be put in place in neighboring states that would be, if not sympathetic about minority rule and apartheid, at least tolerant or afraid of the NP government and, because of their economic vulnerability and their infrastructural links with South Africa, prepared to accept Pretoria and to deal with South Africa "correctly."

Pretoria's leaders reasoned that they could, by coercion, compel these governments to change their policies toward South Africa or, barring that, so discredit and weaken them as to bring about their downfall and replacement by more amenable regimes. Economic threats and pressures were included as parts of the hawkish package. The hard-line position occasionally alternated with offers of treaties of nonaggression, economic linkages and investments, invitations and calls for meetings, and deals—in other words, anything that would seek to legitimize the apartheid regime and reintegrate Pretoria into the mainstream of normal regional relations. (But the stick was always in evidence, as a fallback policy rather than an opening gambit.) Over the years, Pretoria preferred the use of proxies rather than direct South African involvement, although it never completely abandoned the latter technique. In either case, violent means reflect an era of South African foreign policy during which the security establishment was able to enlarge and consolidate its role in central government decisionmaking.

The overall effects of South Africa's "total national strategy" toward its neighbors have been horribly costly. The Commonwealth's report on destabilization estimates that the bill since 1980 amounts to at least $45 billion. Some estimates range up to $60 billion. Beyond the financial costs, some 4 million people have been displaced by the fighting and South Africa's punitive raids, and many (perhaps half the population of Mozambique and Angola) are threatened with hunger. The war-related death toll may be as high as 1.5 million. Direct military action, the disruption of the production and distribution of food, the disruption of education, and the destruction of health facilities and immunization programs all contribute to the human tragedy. Mozambique suffered and still suffers the most damage. Renamo, South Africa's proxy in Mozambique, is barbaric and ruthless in its operations and choice of targets. Smaller areas of Angola are nearly as badly plundered and destroyed, although UNITA does at least make an effort to appeal to popular support in regions where it is dominant. Generally, however, in the areas in which South African and South African–assisted military groups operated, the people suffered terribly. No estimate of lives and economic costs can tell the full story.

As the military success of proxy groups took its toll and South Africa's desire to gain international acceptance sharpened, a marked reduction of reliance on pure force occurred near the end of Botha's tenure and into the de Klerk years. South Africa's regional policy now seems more attuned to the wider international picture. Hence Pretoria seems increasingly amenable to a regional accommodation.

The diplomatic process leading to the independence of Namibia in March 1990 has a long and often frustrating history. One gets the impression that although Pretoria appeared prepared to talk, it resisted any terms of settlement on Angola and Namibia and tried, as much as was possible, to lay blame for a lack of resolution at the doors of SWAPO, the Angolan government, Cuba, or the Western powers. So its dual policy of stick and carrot, sometimes called "thump and talk," sought to delay change; and if change became unavoidable, it sought to empower institutions and politicians submissive to South African pressure and manipulation. But the policy didn't entirely work.

By 1988, the objective conditions facing South Africa in southwestern Africa forced Pretoria to amend its line. The military picture in the region showed signs of deteriorating as far as South Africa was concerned. South Africa's much-publicized military defeat or costly stalemate (depending on who is doing the analysis) at Cuito Cuanavale in late 1987 and early 1988 set the mood. The direct confrontation between Angolan forces, reinforced by Cubans, and UNITA/South African troops raised the fighting to more intense levels. But the shifting military balance contributed to accelerated diplomatic discussion and eventually to a negotiated settlement for the region. South Africa's combat losses, its realization that its theretofore unchallenged control of the air had been ended, and the presence of Cuban troops so close to the Namibian border moved Pretoria to negotiate in earnest. Angola, too, wearied of the hostilities. The Soviet Union, which became keen to cut back on its costly commitments beyond its normal defense perimeter, encouraged Luanda to take steps to end the conflict.

In January 1988, a breakthrough came after the arrival and deployment of additional Cuban troops. U.S. Assistant Secretary of State for Africa Chester Crocker responded favorably to Angola's proposal that Cuba formally join talks. Angola and Cuba were prepared to negotiate a rapid withdrawal of Cuban troops if the United States would mediate and try to convince South Africa to grant independence for Namibia and end its military operations in Angola.

Talks began in London in May and were followed by meetings of representatives from the four countries (Angola, Cuba, South Africa, and the United States) in Cairo, Brazzaville, New York, and Geneva. In August, at Geneva, South Africa announced its readiness to begin implementing the UN plan for Namibian independence as embodied in Resolution 435 and the withdrawal of SADF forces from Angola by mid-1989—if, in return, Angola and Cuba would agree to an identical timetable for the withdrawal of all Cuban troops. A regional cease-fire was also arranged, although UNITA said that it would not observe it and SWAPO, though not formally included in the talks, said it would. Soon thereafter, South Africa ended its assistance to UNITA.

The United States, however, took up where South Africa left off, committing some $50 million to UNITA in 1990 and thereby undermining the cease-fire it ostensibly had worked so patiently to achieve. Apparently U.S. aid to UNITA is a product of internal partisan politics in the United States, with elements on the right of the Republican Party unwilling to abandon a movement that they insist is anticommunist and in direct conflict with a government avowedly Marxist and being supported by the socialist bloc. But many in the administration (in the State Department, the intelligence community, and the White House) feel that aid to UNITA runs counter to the overall aims of stabilizing the region and weaning putatively socialist regimes away from the socialist camp. Persistent violations of the cease-fire agreement, however, failed to destroy either the positive movement toward Namibian independence or the Cuban and South African troop withdrawals.

A crucial accord was reached in New York on December 22, 1988. The three parties (South Africa, Angola, and Cuba) agreed to begin implementing the UN peace plan on April 1, 1989. Despite a terrible opening to the process, in which SWAPO forces trying to cross the border into Namibia were ambushed and killed by South African forces, elections were held peacefully in November 1989. SWAPO gained a 57 percent majority and, in cooperation with other parties, drafted a constitution and saw Namibia through to independence.

Simultaneously, the de Klerk government took major domestic initiatives. It released from prison key ANC leaders (including Nelson Mandela). Parties long opposed to apartheid were unbanned (i.e., permitted to function openly and legally), and preliminary talks between the ANC and government were announced. The world praised these steps and called for more, such as the further release of political prisoners, an end to the state of emergency, and firmer control of the police, who had been using undue violence to break up rallies and protest demonstrations. But the optimism set in motion has been marred by the continued provocative behavior of the security establishment as well as by extensive Black political violence, especially in Natal province and in the townships on the Reef near Johannesburg. The South African Police (SAP), or segments thereof, seem determined to inhibit open political activity by leftist parties, despite the government's announced policy of unbanning parties. They have provoked bloody confrontations with massed demonstrators and have shown favoritism and given aid to conservative factions in the intra-Black conflicts. Private groups based in South Africa, and possibly units of the SADF as well, still assist Renamo in Mozambique.

Government disclaims these policies but seems unable or unwilling either to take steps to terminate support for Mozambique's enemies or to clamp down on wildcat police action. Despite this scenario, however, there is clearly a different, more upbeat atmosphere in the region since de Klerk came to power. The promise of region-wide peace seems alive.

Part of the reason South Africa and apartheid have been such hot international issues is that South Africa insisted on defending apartheid by being engaged militarily beyond its borders. South Africa itself became a threat to the regional peace as well as to the good order of Black South Africa. Its stance, in turn, enabled the socialist bloc to become involved in the regional picture. As states vulnerable to South Africa's pressures and incursions sought help, and as the Western powers failed to respond, the socialist bloc happily saw these events as "windows of opportunity." The timing of the recent peace initiatives, however, has been fortuitous. The rise of Mikhail Gorbachev, the preoccupation of the Soviet state with domestic crises (economic, structural, and ethnic), Gorbachev's commitment to glasnost, and his "new thinking" on foreign policy issues led the Soviet Union to play a central role in helping to resolve the Angola/Namibia stalemate.

Militarily, the region's profile has been lowered. Today the transitional process is largely seen as a diplomatic and domestic issue now that the principal parties (the NP government and the ANC) are directly addressing their outstanding differences. Pretoria behaves officially as if the agenda for change is open. Unofficially, segments of the established elite behave as if little has changed and they intend to retain control as before. The outside world focuses on the official posture and praises de Klerk and Mandela. But insiders have to live with the reality of unofficial regime violence and dominance, and with Black-on-Black violence precipitated in part by regime neglect, favoritism, and instigation. For as long as a regional order can be maintained (and Mozambique and Angola are thus far not ready to say that an acceptable order has been established), South Africa can be expected to become less of an international concern.

REINING IN THE SECURITY ESTABLISHMENT

During the past three decades we have witnessed several fundamental changes in South Africa's security situation. At first, during the 1960s, South Africa's relative strength (domestically in terms of police power and regionally in military power) and its relative economic weight provided South Africa with a virtually unobstructed ability to impose its will. South Africa's advantage was not so much a function of its strength as of the relative physical weakness of Pretoria's enemies. South Africa and its political leaders seemed to have purpose, organization, and a willingness to use force, ruthlessly if necessary to achieve their ends. In contrast, apartheid's enemies were divided, preoccupied with economic and state survival, and disorganized. They disagreed on how best to deal with the realities of apartheid power, and they could not spare the resources needed to press their aims. South Africa was a military Gulliver among Lilliputians without means and in disarray.

What kept South Africa in line was an international community determined to limit the violent and aggressive conduct of apartheid foreign policy. Also instrumental was the realization by the South African government and its critics at home that the country's military resources were not boundless and that to dissipate them in battles beyond the borders, while militarily successful, would be politically and economically disastrous. It is clear, however, that on the domestic front Pretoria was prepared to use all means at its disposal to destroy its enemies and to hold power. South Africans after the Sharpeville massacre were transformed into a sullen mass. Those who did not conform either were forced into exile or paid heavily for their independence of mind.

In the 1970s, and then with even greater speed and effect in the 1980s, the challenges against apartheid mounted. Moreover, they came to be backed by resources, organizational direction, and assistance from beyond Africa. The Soweto uprising and the brutal suppression of what had begun as school protests and widened into a nationwide resistance focused attention again on South Africa's internal order. But by that time the coup in Portugal in April 1974, followed by the independence of Angola and Mozambique, tilted the strategic distribution of power in the region against South Africa. Zimbabwe's independence in 1980, after the successful conduct of a protracted guerrilla war for independence and majority rule, shifted the balance still further. Advantages that South Africa had secured in the past by guile, diplomacy, and economic leverage now had to be imposed forcefully and maintained at inordinate costs. Increasingly the security establishment had to be fed and nurtured and favored in state councils. Despite the steady buildup of the SADF and the projection of that power into neighboring states, South Africa saw its hinterland slipping away. It may have been winning battles, but it was losing the war. Though militarily powerful, it was becoming more and more politically bankrupt. Its more perceptive leaders watched this outcome develop and pondered how to parlay their strength into political credibility.

Meanwhile, South Africa's economy suffered as its domestic tranquillity, always an imposed order, unraveled. Black resistance movements again sent out roots. The ANC and SWAPO were able to infiltrate, engage in what the ANC called "armed propaganda," and test the regime. Voices long silent within South Africa took heart from the changing regional picture. Borrowed from the cries of Frelimo in Mozambique, "Viva!" entered the vocabulary of South African resistance, as popular opposition began to coalesce around the United Democratic Front and later the Mass Democratic Movement. Despite South Africa's mobilization and militarization, the war to defend apartheid was not winnable. Finally, late in the Botha years, some within the civilian hierarchy began to realize the futility of a policy predicated principally on coercion.

Through the years the security establishment and its armed forces grew in size and importance. The apartheid regime has created a sorcerer's apprentice of sorts. The security establishment became a political force throwing its weight around in white politics. It has a certain perspective on political problems and, on the surface, has few counterforces in South African society. Who can rein in the armed forces and police, and how? Civilian control of the armed forces is imperative for any serious steps toward long-term resolution of South Africa's puzzle.

F. W. de Klerk, unlike P. W. Botha, has had little background among securocrats. He is a lifelong party man, and if he is to assert full control of government, he must displace Botha's appointees at various levels of the security apparatus. Almost from his assumption of the state presidency after the September 1989 election (he had been acting state president for only a few weeks before that, following Botha's August resignation), he sought to establish his authority over the securocrats. It has not been easy.

Opposition to the securocrats had, in fact, been expressed within government throughout the Botha years. The Department of Foreign Affairs, as well as various economic and social departments of government, had sought to offset the security dominance. They realized that a heavy-handed imposition of armed will made their jobs of relating abroad virtually impossible. On occasion, SADF operations seemed calculated to sabotage the diplomatic process in Angola. In some military circles, Foreign Minister R. F. Botha was regarded as a traitor. Given these deep cleavages in high government councils, no wonder it was not easy to determine exactly who was responsible for regional and, at times, domestic policy.

A kind of ebb and flow had characterized South Africa's regional policies. Unable to achieve its aims economically and diplomatically, Pretoria took military steps. Eventually, a target government became unable to resist the pressure and called for accommodation and perhaps even offered concessions. Accords were reached, sometimes publicly, sometimes secretly. But the interests of the vulnerable Black goverments and those of apartheid South Africa were fundamentally incompatible. Sooner or later the modus vivendi broke down, thus leading again to economic warfare and possibly another round of military operations. And so it went.

The futility of this conflictual policy became apparent during the 1980s. South Africa's decision to seek agreement on Angola and Namibia represented a major setback for the securocrats. Ironically, their military effectiveness contributed to the protracted stalemate that raised the costs to the principal combatants and hence drove them to the bargaining table. But the overall impact has been to precipitate SADF withdrawal from Angola and, with the independence of Namibia, from that country, too. The result has been lower budgets and lower force levels. The SADF brass is not thrilled with the SADF's forced withdrawal and insists that it did not lose at Cuito Cuanavale. But they do appreciate that they were outgunned in Angola (though not in Namibia) and that they need to modernize and regroup their forces.

Other steps to rein in the SADF entail scrapping the National Security Management System (NSMS), terminating assistance to UNITA (most of which had been managed by the SADF), reducing the terms of military obligation for compulsory National Service, investigating and curbing the activities of death squads operating under SADF auspices, and closing some secret bases where units of proxy forces from neighboring countries and from Black factions within South Africa had been trained and sheltered. Military intelligence has been reduced in significance in relation to the National Intelligence Service externally and the security police internally. Both are civilian agencies. The budget announced in early 1990 showed a marked reduction of SADF and Armscor allotments— perhaps as much as a 20 percent cut in defense spending. The cuts include disbanding or scaling down various navy and air force formations, selling redundant equipment, postponing or canceling armaments projects and testing, reducing operating costs, laying off civilian workers in the defense department and at Armscor, and reducing National Service from two years to twelve months. Some of these steps have not been instituted with the intent of weakening or reining in the defense establishment in the domestic political arena. Rather, they have been designed to reduce budgets and unpopular service assignments at a time of reduced need for the SADF and of added demands on the state. But the net effect has been to lessen the political importance of the securocrats, to narrow their range of policy involvement, and to rely on less coercive instruments of policy.

The once-secret counterrevolutionary NSMS was introduced by P. W. Botha in 1986. It had been planned as a pervasive network of committees, from the high-level State Security Council where all policy applying to security (defined most expansively) was decided, to the 9 regional Joint Management Centres (JMCs), to the 82 sub-JMCs and 320 mini-JMCs. All were dominated by the SADF and, to a lesser extent, by police officers. In sum, the NSMS constituted an alternative government/

bureaucracy that would manage public affairs at all levels in times of strife and emergency. In fact, it operated in peacetime, too. Its various committees intended to nip unrest in the bud by taking the measures necessary to defuse potentially explosive conditions. At times and in selected locales, these committees replaced or superseded elected local bodies, especially in Black townships where local councillors and officials refused to serve or were discredited or forced to resign.

In November 1989, President de Klerk downgraded the State Security Council to the level of the other cabinet subcommittees. He also scrapped the JMCs, replacing them with Regional Coordinating Committees under civilian control. The sub-JMCs were also abolished and the mini-JMCs were turned into local coordinating committees, to meet only when necessary. The main aim has been to confirm the cabinet as the "highest policymaking and coordinating power" in government. In power only three months at the time, de Klerk realized that as long as the securocrats were operating behind the scenes, serious efforts to seek accommodation with the Black resistance would be held to ransom.

Similar steps to control the police are in the works. They include a partial ending of the State of Emergency in February 1990 and a total ending in October, the release of many but not all detainees and political prisoners, the unbanning of antiapartheid resistance organizations, and investigations into violent deaths in detention. There is evidence that some police resist these changes and have provoked violence with demonstrators and among ANC supporters. Others seem to behave at times as if the bannings were still in force. And many still identified with conservative and reactionary white parties and movements and with collaborative Black politicians. In the intra-Zulu warfare in Natal province, and in the Transvaal where white paramilitary neofascist groups operate openly and provocatively, the police have been seen to favor the Inkatha fighters of Chief Buthelezi, other provocateurs, and demonstrators from the Afrikaner Weerstandsbeweging (a right-wing paramilitary group fashioned after the Nazi Brown Shirts). In this context, analysts question whether de Klerk's government is really in charge.

CONCLUSION

In these troubled times of potentially rapid and extensive transition, it is imperative to know which side or faction in domestic politics is being backed by the arms of state, especially in regard to government's apparent program for maintaining order in the midst of change and reformist concession. The fact is that the security establishment, which under P. W. Botha was so favored in status, funding, and power, fears being eclipsed or divided. Yet its obedient cooperation is vital in these difficult times, for people are being asked, and are often compelled, to make concessions against their perceived interests and will. Can governmental agencies advantaged by the previous regime be expected to enforce laws and regulations that contribute to their own demotion? Would it have made sense for Lenin and Trotsky to have depended upon the Czarist officer corps to lead and organize the Red Army? What if Washington had expected the British Red Coats to defend the revolution after their surrender at Yorktown?

In our own era, the dilemmas of the Philippines under Corazon Aquino and Nicaragua under Violetta Chamorro illustrate the need to assert control over the armed forces. To be sure, the changes that have thus far taken place in South Africa, and those envisioned by de Klerk in his most euphoric and ambitious moods, are by no means as unsettling to the status quo as those instituted during the American or Russian revolutions. But transitional processes can assume a dynamic of their own that outpaces the best-laid plans of those who initiate them. Indeed, ill-conceived reforms can drift into revolutions. So the basic principle holds: The forces of the *ancien régime* are not the most committed instruments of a new order, whether reformist or revolutionary. When they possess the physical power to frustrate those plans, transitional politics becomes awkward at best.

We need to know how far de Klerk is prepared to go and how he can be compelled to go even farther, faster. Various components of the security establishment have different thresholds of toleration toward change. A lashing back by one or more risks upsetting the van of change. And yet there seems to be no one in a position to counter the armed forces. Is people power sufficiently organized and united to propel the revolution onward? In these exacting times, virtually all options are open in the free-for-all struggle to shape South Africa's future.

SEVEN

□ □ □

Conclusion: South Africa's Future and the World

One's reading of the future of South Africa as an issue confronting the international community or parts thereof is itself based on one's sense of whether the process of reform leading to power sharing (as the white regime prefers) or to a transfer of power or majority rule in a unitary state based on one person/one vote (as the ANC and other progressive activists desire) can be sustained. One may justifiably assume that the transition, no matter what the outcome, cannot be totally peaceful. There are already such deep cleavages within the Black and white communities, and the divisions between the races are deeper still. Such differences make it almost impossible for even the most respected and popular leaders to guarantee discipline and obedience among all for whom they purport to speak. Even in the most upbeat reading of South Africa's short-term future, violence and coercion will play an important part. And yet, in another respect, the prospect of widespread violence is precisely what motivates and propels rational leaders toward compromise, concession, and accommodation. Advocates of reason are, in a perverse way, strengthened by the probability that if they fail, the forces of irrationality would be ascendant.

Even in transition, South Africa's circumstances are unusual, if not unique. The South African government appears to be ready to participate in talks leading to significant change (a revolutionary transfer of power is not a part of their stated agenda) even though that government is not at the point of collapse. Nor are its armed forces necessarily deserting the regime. Although there are considerable numbers of Blacks in the SADF and the SAP, few seem ready to defect to fight for Black majority rule. If anything, the white members of these organizations are drifting toward the far right, toward those who regard compromise or negotiation as treason. If the regime faces a sudden threat, it is from those traditionally identified as supporters of the apartheid state, the violent white neofascists.

But the South African government, though politically on the ropes, is not disintegrating as did the communist governments of eastern Europe or the Marcos government in the Philippines. Nor has Pretoria's government been worn down by war, as were the regimes in Zimbabwe or Portugal because of the latter's wars in Africa or even the divisive governments in Nicaragua or El Salvador. Nor is South Africa so dependent on a single outside power or bloc of states as to force Pretoria to bend to its concerted demands. Nevertheless, a case can be made for offering concessions now and negotiating from a perceived sense of strength. Unlike the popular uprising from 1984 to 1986, when the regime was directly threatened with a domestic civil uprising and with the loss of control over certain townships, the situation today (though still extremely violent) is less of a threat to the regime per se. Indeed, the internecine Black strife provided a ready excuse for maintaining the state of emergency, for deploying soldiers and armed police in selected hot spots, and for further delaying the process of reform. The state of emergency was in force in strife-torn Natal and in selected townships near Johannesburg until October 1990.

Rather, the South African government has been driven to the negotiating table by a combination of pressures, no one of which would be sufficient in itself to carry the day. These pressures emanate from the global community (especially its focused economic sanctions and its punishing exclusion of South Africa from normal diplomatic and social intercourse); from the costly war in Namibia/Angola, which showed little prospect of resolution as a military encounter and much prospect of draining South Africa of treasure and eventually blood; from the renewed life of the domestic Black resistance, which simply would not be silenced or cowed; and from the government's realization that to impose silence would only make total South Africa's economic isolation in the world. It was a classic, hurting stalemate, in which each of the major poles came to realize that although it may be strong enough to prevent an imposed solution by its opponents, it was not strong enough to win. By 1989, each side had, I believe, recognized its own limitations and calculated that the time had arrived to explore alternatives. But that exploration has just begun, and the elements of violence and irrationality are still all too evident.

THREE SCENARIOS

Crystal-balling South Africa is therefore filled with imponderables. The range of possible outcomes is wide. To establish some order to the discussion, one might pose three possible scenarios that, while radically different, cover the general directions of change if not the detailed ingredients or sequences that might emerge.

The first we might regard as the *optimistic future.* In it the process of negotiation, started under the rubric of "talks about talks" and "creating the climate for negotiations," leads eventually to majority rule. In such an optimistic scenario, a formula is worked out for providing minorities with a sense of security and with workable legal safeguards against majority domination and exploitation. But it is unlikely that this process would be flawless or entirely bloodless. There is simply too much psychological energy in South Africa, too much fear and hatred, and too much to lose materially to think that talks would be linear and lacking occasional setbacks or breaks.

South Africa's political culture has long disparaged moderation and compromise. Given the historically rigid political separation of the races and the great gaps in the distribution of power, an individual leader who counseled less than total power for his constituency was in danger of losing his following. Political power was founded on the exercise of coercion and intimidation, and that exercise contributed to strong emotions, hardened positions, and the rejection of conciliatory attitudes and views. White survival and Black redress insist upon group solidarity. In this social atmosphere, bridge builders are seldom welcomed or appreciated. Indeed, throughout the 1970s and the 1980s, a form of Gresham's Law of militarism applied whereby the cooperative and negotiable were driven out by the assertive and violent. The heavy-handed exercise of power was glorified; the military metaphor replaced the conciliatory and diplomatic.

But these deep-seated tendencies led to bloody stalemate, economic malaise, and hopelessness. South Africa was indeed fortunate to break from the negative spiral in which it seemed trapped. But that escape is none too secure. Trust is difficult to establish after centuries of mistrust, misunderstanding, and exploitation.

South African whites are among the most heavily armed people in the world, and firearms are increasingly becoming available among Blacks. There are segments of the white population and others in the Black community to whom compromise is regarded as surrender and reason is weakness. More and more often, they reject the leadership of either the ANC or the NP. Neo-Nazi elements exist in dozens of small groups. A few are relatively well prepared, and all are committed to the employment of violence to prevent the ascendance of Black political power. Some individual members are well placed in the police and the armed forces. Groups such as the Afrikaner Weerstandsbeweging (AWB), a paramilitary organization heavily into flags, uniforms, and neo-Nazi symbolism, are gaining in support. "We talk with microphones and loudspeakers," says its leader, Eugene TerreBlanche, "but you will have to act through the barrel of a gun. You will have to kill." The AWB membership is estimated at 100,000. On the lunatic fringe are a bevy of smaller groups, some truly prepared to begin a war for white resistance. They all make heroes of those who have taken up arms against Blacks or who preach white supremacy.

In contrast, various Black extremists talk of driving whites into the sea or of expelling white "settlers." Others more narrowly speak for national, ethnic, and tribal forces. Still others, largely a criminal element, gain from the social disruption that race war entails.

Unless these groups and individuals can be discredited, isolated, weakened, and eventually disarmed, the optimistic future scenario holds little promise. For these elements have the capacity to destroy trust and fragile compromise. By staking out polar positions, and by forcing the indecisive or insecure to choose sides, they are in a position to disrupt delicate negotiations and experimental agreements.

An optimistic transition also requires the minimization of economic damage and a sense of confidence in the future of the negotiated settlement. In this process, which could take years to bring about, foreign governments, organizations, and businesses must stand ready to assist because they are convinced that the key actors in the negotiations are determined to make the negotiated order work. If peace, trust, and confidence are the products of a positive negotiation and transition process, great success is possible for South Africa.

In this setting the economic viability of South Africa, as a respected and accepted international actor, would be ensured. The country could then resume its place as a regional engine of development. According to Westerners who see an optimistic outcome to the end of apartheid, the economic development of South Africa has been artificially retarded for the last fifteen years or so by the domestic costs of maintaining apartheid and the world's refusal to finance the apartheid state and the enterprises there. Consequently, as they see it, an end to apartheid would lead almost automatically to rapid economic growth.

First, the costs of maintaining apartheid would be ended. The bloated bureaucracy would be streamlined and the duplication of managerial layers stopped. Military and police budgets would be reduced. Conscription for white men would no longer be necessary, and they would be free to pursue their careers without interruption. The costs associated with sanctions—for example, the premium prices paid to evade the petroleum embargo and embargoes on other imported products, and the lower prices accepted on South Africa's exports because of sanctions— would be ended. And the same patterns of higher costs for capital imports (premium for risk, as it were) would likely be reduced, especially if the transition is brought about peacefully.

Second, and just as important, an end to apartheid would lead to a more efficient allocation of resources. Blacks would have greater op- portunities and incentives to work, to be trained and educated, and to consume. Presumably, market considerations would become more central to the labor market. In this context, economic growth would lead to expanded employment, thus lowering the chances for civil unrest. But such changes would obviously depend on the policies and programs of the majority government. Provided that skilled whites stay, at least until their technical and managerial skills could be replaced and acquired by the Black population—and, here, the Zimbabwe experience provides some reassurance (compared to Mozambique or Angola), especially given the considerably larger core of white citizens in South Africa—the transition would be tolerably smooth. In this scenario, a peaceful transition to postapartheid, coupled with rapid economic development and growth, is the key.

By contrast, a *pessimistic scenario* would lead in one of several directions marked by widespread violence, economic breakdown, and social collapse. The NP government, for instance, might lose its nerve and revert to the rigid coercive policies of its predecessors. But this is an order few Blacks are prepared to accept without a renewed armed struggle, an order that simply cannot work. In a more extreme situation, the NP could be discredited in the white polity and the white backlash could bring to power a neofascist party determined to destroy Black resistance. Some of these neofascist groups have been described in the previous pages. Certain white supremacists have threatened a "new Boer War." They have already accused de Klerk of having "capitulated" to Blacks. Their demonstrations have been large and bellicose. And smaller, even less responsible, vigilante groups are already in place. In 1990, a government defense force arsenal was raided by white extremists. The NP government recognized the threat from this quarter and in the same year responded by withdrawing weapons from rural commandos, a traditional part of South Africa's armed forces reserve.

Any such white organized fury would assuredly precipitate the re- emergence of Black armed resistance and easily lead to an all-out civil war reminiscent of anarchic and confused Lebanon rather than the neater dichotomies of Vietnam or Zimbabwe. Should this occur, the outside world would double its efforts to force Pretoria to reopen negotiations. But little change overall would be brought about before a good deal of South Africa has been laid to waste and tens of thousands have died. White extremists have been warning about this Armageddon future for years. In the past, many people regarded their words as a threat and a bargaining ploy to demonstrate their determination not to budge or be pushed around. In the current state of white and Black political consciousness and mobilization, however, this scenario is far from impossible.

Another pessimistic scenario involves the *fragmentation of the Black community*, which might occur either before or during negotiations on the future constitutional dispensation. The ANC, in this scenario, is still not able to speak for all Black South Africans. After all, most of the Black parties and antiapartheid organizations were legalized only as of February 1990. To expect them to organize throughout the country, at the grassroots level, in the face of official noncooperation if not harrassment and antagonism, is unrealistic. Moreover, as an underground, illegal party operating in exile for the last thirty years, the ANC fell into habits of decisionmaking and political action that were sometimes less than democratic. Democratic practices were a luxury that would likely jeopardize their security. In important parts of the country, the ANC cannot be sure that its decisions will be followed. The most obvious focus of possible dissension would be in Natal, among the Zulus; but similar discontents might be expressed in other homelands, among the trade unionists and "comrades" in the townships, or among lawless elements or traditional and entrenched political bosses.

Already there are those who question whether the "old men" in the ANC, such as Oliver Tambo, Alfred Nzo, and even Mandela himself, have lost touch with the situation on the ground. In any case, within this scenario, the white government, even with the collaboration of the ANC, would be unable to restore order. Whites would panic and, lacking confidence in any Black leadership, would either refuse to cooperate with government or flee South Africa. The outside world would not understand or tolerate Black-on-Black violence, no matter what its causes, just as Westerners have been put off by "necklacing." So the West might be tempted to relax the pressures on white-ruled Pretoria and allow it to be more forceful in asserting its political claims. Law and order would again become the guidelines, and the result would be either civil war or some form of protracted and very bloody unrest.

Even if a majority government were ushered to power, and particularly if it did not achieve power by relatively peaceful means, it might be extremely insecure and defensive. Consequently, it might threaten human and civil rights, and try to rule by fiat and coercion. Such a future might lead to a succession of dictatorships and to a pattern of "extractive" politics whereby those in power seek to use their public positions for private material gain.

A third scenario lies between the optimistic and the pessimistic scenarios. A *middle-of-the-road future* for South Africa would entail the achievement of Black power and majority rule, but at potentially debilitating costs. In such circumstances, Black divisions would be widened and white resistance extensive. Yet both would be kept at manageable or acceptable levels. But the time scale for the transition to majority rule would be greatly extended, the numbers of casualties and deaths in the struggle would be great, resentments would deepen, the economy would suffer because little new investment will occur, and a steady white flight would reduce South Africa's pool of vital skills. Black power is a reality, but at the price of rewarding the most militant in the movement and deferring the rewards so long worked for. Such a scenario would set South Africa back decades in both economic and social recovery.

The competitive world of capitalist development is sensitive to the vagaries of political instability, even to a lack of confidence in the regime or its government. Black government, in and of itself, will not ensure a sufficient supply of new capital and technology to South Africa. To be sure, South Africa's minerals will presumably be in steady demand. But investments in mines require an extended lead time before they can be expected to render a return. Accordingly, the capitalist world's perception of the new regime is an important ingredient in that regime's success.

A majoritarian government that fails to capture the support of foreign or local business interests is thus unable to ensure the economic performance necessary to enable it to provide services and meet expectations for very long. Jobs, government revenues, credit, a stable banking and financial environment, trust, confidence, and hope are important to any future regime. Limping along is almost as bad as falling, for it fails to contribute to an atmosphere of promise.

Transitions to majority rule in Africa have never been easy. All conditions must be right: a near-perfect confluence of leadership, resources, climate, economy, foreign cooperation, purpose, and goodwill. Any added complication, such as a bitter and hateful struggle, only compounds the challenge. South Africa, despite its long record of exploitation and denial of Black rights and opportunity, still possesses a reservoir of goodwill that is hard for outsiders to comprehend. How long it will last should the struggle reescalate is difficult to predict.

POLICY GUIDES TO A SOUTH AFRICA ON THE MOVE

It is hard to fashion policy in such a state of flux. It is harder still when we consider that there is little consensus in the United States, least of all in the West, on how best to deal with South Africa. The best advice is not especially original or profound—it is the wisdom of wait and see.

The sanctions that are in place appear to have had a serious effect on the South African economy and psyche. To the extent that they have been conscientiously implemented, they have worked. Testimony to that impact can now be derived from many and diverse quarters. The heightened sanctions of the last five years and the other steps taken to isolate and ostracize Pretoria have seemed to encourage Black resistance, to undermine NP confidence and rigidity, and to complement the efforts of those within South Africa seeking to end apartheid. But it is important to keep the pressure on South Africa; and, to that end, steps should be taken to close the remaining loopholes in sanctions policies and the enabling legislation by which they are enforced. Where these laws have been only casually enforced, governments must carry through on their stated policies. Do nothing to relieve the stress on Pretoria, but be ready to consider reducing sanctions and isolation only after positive and irreversible steps have been taken to end minority rule.

Another positive element is that western and Soviet-bloc interests seem to have coincided somewhat in southern Africa. The superpowers are on a roll of collaboration, not conflict; and apparently they do not want differences in southern Africa to halt that trend. Some have suggested that the process leading to resolution of the Namibian dispute and the independence of Namibia itself might serve as a model for the settlement of other outstanding conflicts in the region. The Renamo-Frelimo War in Mozambique, the problem of national reconciliation in Angola, and the South African issue beg for resolution.

On the latter issue, behind-the-scenes persuasion is needed to force the South African government to seize authoritative control, if it can, over the SADF and the police and especially over the dissident elements therein. Right-wing members of these arms of state must be relieved of duty and progressively replaced by individuals from the majority community who are prepared to enforce liberalizing laws and regulations as they are enacted. Such a transition within the armed forces would also facilitate the integration of the fighting forces of the two sides in a postapartheid South Africa. Already there have been consultations on these integrative issues.

It would be helpful if outside powers prepared themselves to play positive roles as intermediaries in the negotiation/transition process.

Expectations that a resolution for South Africa will come soon are unduly high, higher than at any time since the British-sponsored Lancaster House talks in 1979 ushered in an independent Zimbabwe. And since the well-publicized release of Mandela and the unbanning of various antiapartheid movements, they have risen even higher. Before the ANC and the South African government began meeting openly, the Soviet Union offered to arrange meetings between the two major parties. But Pretoria declined the offer. Nonetheless, third parties (whether other governments, individuals, or organizations) can supplement the negotiation process and be helpful elsewhere by providing good offices or by acting as mediators, arbitrators, or facilitators.

Superpower collaboration in this area is possible, now that both the United States and the USSR seem to prefer a peaceful political settlement. Certainly Moscow no longer favors armed revolution in South Africa. It talks of preserving South Africa's viable economy and of coming to terms with ethnicity and group rights. The Soviet government has even started opening lines of communication with the government and among white liberals. In the past, U.S. interests were predominantly economic and strategic, whereas Soviet interests stressed the political and the ideological. The USSR employed chiefly military means to bring about its goals. Today, both sides seem to be more pragmatic.

In late 1988, Gorbachev told the UN of the need to "de-ideologiz[e] relations among states." One should not exaggerate the convergence of interests between the United States and the USSR; but considering the situation just five years ago, the next five years could lead to further surprises. The Soviets still exhibit a preference for Marxist friends, and for Americans procapitalist policies provide foreign policy continuity. Competition rather than partnership is still the mode, but both superpowers want to avoid destructive conflict and head-on confrontation. It is the possibility of collaboration that holds such promise for southern Africa.

By offering its good offices, a party may intercede in a dispute or a negotiating process. It brings disputants together and induces them to begin or resume negotiations. A party that mediates goes even further by getting directly involved in the negotiations and by trying to help the contending parties over difficult issues. Other variants of third-party intercession may also be employed. Generally speaking, international organizations such as the UN and the OAU are not ideal venues for negotiation: They are too public and too biased. But they may be useful (as would be the Great Powers) in guaranteeing and legitimizing the terms of a settlement.

The Western powers have not only the economic clout to force Pretoria to find more accommodating ways of dealing with Black demands but also the resources to encourage a resolution. In other words, economic blandishments might be held out to secure concessions and facilitate the imposition of a new regime.

However, the West is not united on specific policy proposals toward South Africa. Within the United States itself, Congress is divided (though not strictly along partisan lines) and the executive branch has been giving mixed signals. The Bush administration seems committed to a bipartisan approach to foreign policy and to gaining African-American support. Yet it also has obligations to business interests, and it fears alienating the right in the Republican Party, which still is burdened with cold war and racial hang-ups. The South African issue seems to trigger both of these complexes. At a broader level, public opinion vacillates— not so much in its opposition to apartheid but in the fervor of its views and commitment, and in its political span of attention. It is not easy for the U.S. government to act effectively without a consensus unless the issue is low profile and insignificant. With South Africa, that is no longer the case.

Policy reflects this confusion. The Comprehensive Anti-Apartheid Act of 1986 is a jumbled piece of Christmas tree legislation with some eighteen different types of sanctions riddled with loopholes apparent to all. So U.S. policy is sometimes contradictory and unclear. Even if the executive branch were entirely committed to expediting revolutionary change in South Africa, it is faced with the unwillingness of four countries—West Germany, the U.K., Japan, and Israel—to follow the uncertain U.S. lead. Together they maintain links with South Africa far greater and more important than those of the United States.

If the West could approach the South African situation from a relatively unified position, such factors as aid, technical assistance, military and security assistance, trade concessions, credits, and investments might contribute to an orderly transition. But the United States does not have an especially good record in helping newly independent African governments, especially those with left or Marxist leanings. The United States' aid record toward Zimbabwe and its 1990 offer of a paltry $500,000 for Namibia (compared to $50 million for UNITA to continue fighting in Angola) have provided the Black majority in South Africa with little hope of a major bailout from the United States.

As we await the negotiations in South Africa to bear fruit, the West can take steps to strengthen democracy and economic development in the remaining part of southern Africa that surrounds South Africa. The economic and military disparities between these countries and South Africa are still significant, and their sense of vulnerability cannot be assuaged by what may be but a temporary South African abatement in its policy of destabilization. By supporting the Black governments that had been the targets of South Africa's aggressive policies, the West can help to establish not only a sense of security but also a few successes in development and race relations elsewhere within the region.

Many South African whites are convinced that Black government invariably leads to economic deterioration, the erosion of civil and political rights, widespread corruption, and the decline of state services. The South African press is full of horror stories of life in Black Africa to the north. But South Africans need to be convinced that, given the right conditions, this disintegrative course is not inevitable or unidirectional. The Southern African Development Coordination Conference (SADCC) provides the organizational vehicle for this regional development effort, and any attempt to strengthen these states vis-à-vis South Africa delivers a message to Pretoria.

There is little that the West can do to alter the balance of power in South Africa itself, or even within the region, at least in the short term. But Western policy must be responsive to initiatives provided by the political and social leaders in the region, insofar as those leads are clear and widely supported. The West, as well, must be supportive of negotiations between the real spokespersons for the key power elements. No longer should the West pretend that co-opted Black "moderates" have an extensive following in South Africa.

Pressure on the regime must be accompanied by pressure on their Black counterparts. As with the settlement in Namibia, the Soviet Union and Black African governments, especially those in the Front Line States, are presumably better situated to persuade the ANC and its allies than is the West. But this is not to say that the West should abandon the revolutionary and progressive parties. Too often in the past, the West has focused on the white elite as the critical factor in any South African resolution. This certainly was the message of NSSM-39 and "constructive engagement." It is time, now, to cultivate links with the majority community and its revolutionary organizations. Strong and disciplined Black organizations contribute to the elicitation of more concessions from the white regime than can Western pressures, although in concert they can accomplish even more.

But the West, in turn, must be prepared to see that Pretoria cooperates. Toward that end, it must thwart and frustrate the military options of Renamo in Mozambique, of UNITA in Angola, of other proxy groups in the region, of South Africa itself, and of the diehard racists in South Africa. It must also reinforce the advocates of cooperation and change. Unfortunately, there are some elements in this equation—white extremists, some Black nationalists around the PAC, local Black political bosses, and some of the comrades—who are less amenable to externally based pressures.

With South Africa, the external community has an opportunity to serve as midwife to a negotiated revolution. Such a process entails the pursuit of a two-channel strategy. First, it must seek to strengthen the hands of the principal revolutionary parties in South Africa, especially by helping them to organize and educate their followers and their enemies to the fact that they are unified and capable of managing a modern state. Their military capabilities will have to be improved too, for the government and extremists to its right are not resting on their weapons. Related to this is the need to bolster the ability of the Front Line States to survive South African economic and military sway.

Second, and at the same time, the foreign powers can try to facilitate a peaceful, negotiated settlement by employing the various techniques discussed throughout this book. In the process, the majority community must be persuaded to provide the minority communities with reliable safeguards for their economic and political rights. But this may not be easy, given the ruthless means by which whites have retained power and exploited the majority. Confidence-building measures are necessary if both communities are to feel protected and inclined to concede "nonnegotiable" points.

The pace of change has quickened in South Africa, and the foreign powers must do their best to keep the transition process on track. As each successive bargaining proposal and gambit is made public, it must be weighed and evaluated. As the major parties in the negotiations are South African, it is not the West's task to address each scheme as it is advanced. Nor is it my task to make such evaluations here. Rather, the West must examine the various foreign policy instruments and means of leverage that have been used against Pretoria and the antiapartheid forces, and determine why, how, and to what effect they have been employed.

A vital threshold was reached in South Africa in the summer and fall of 1989. Government saw that it had to go beyond the "change without really changing" mode favored by P. W. Botha. The Black resistance had taken on a life that government policy, no matter how harsh, could not still. Sensing this efflorescent revolutionary power, the two sides seemed ready to move toward talks. Years of negation seemed to fall away. South Africa is in the midst of that process now. It is taking the first awkward steps toward the bargaining table. The requisite compromises that will follow must be sold to sometimes divided, sometimes doubting, sometimes hostile constituencies. It would appear that, for the present, none of the parties want outsiders to play an active hands-on role in the negotiation process. They seem to reject a contemporary version of Camp David in which a powerful president, prime minister, or UN secretary general puts his or her prestige on the line to hammer out agreements.

Instead, the parties seem ready for a less meddlesome, but no less supportive, role from outside parties. Keep the process on track, they urge us, without dictating the direction, pace, or character of that process. But the bottom line is that South Africa is undergoing a period of such rapid flux that few outsiders are ready to overcommit for fear of being too soon out of touch with newly emerging centers of power. Because the fulcrum of debate ultimately lies within South Africa, the struggle for freedom and democracy there lies not in external involvement (although that can help) but inside South Africa itself. Outsiders should take their cues from the primary actors in the contest, not from foreign interests with an agenda of their own.

□ □ □

Discussion Questions

CHAPTER ONE

1. Apartheid is one among several possible schemes by which a multinational state may be structured. Precisely what is apartheid, and why is it so universally regarded as an unacceptable form of governance? Is territorial partition inherently wrong? Under what circumstances would territorial partition make sense for racially or ethnically diverse states?

2. In what ways is apartheid essentially an economic phenomenon?

3. How can a population of approximately 4.5 million whites keep an estimated population of 25 million Black people under control? Discuss the various methods by which dominance is maintained in South Africa.

CHAPTER TWO

1. It has been said that international norms and values are continually changing. Discuss such changes in the twentieth century and show how these changes have affected South Africa's international standing. What changes currently in progress can you discern?

2. In what ways has U.S. foreign policy been supportive of the South African government? Why has the United States been reluctant to back revolution in South Africa without reservation? To what extent have other governments in the world shared Washington's misgivings?

3. To what extent has Pretoria sought to open links with Black governments in Africa? What are its motives for such policies? Why has it had difficulties being accepted in Africa and elsewhere in the Third World?

CHAPTER THREE

1. In what ways have South African policies and apartheid been cold war or East-West issues? Who gains by regarding South African politics in a cold war context and who suffers? Why?

2. What is the rationalization for regarding apartheid as an international rather than strictly a South African domestic concern?

3. What larger generalizations can a student of international law draw from the experiences of South Africa at the United Nations, its various agencies and organs, and the International Court of Justice?

4. Why can it be argued that in the late 1980s the South African crisis became "ripe for resolution"? Under what circumstances can South Africa become less important and hence less "ripe for resolution"?

CHAPTER FOUR

1. Where does South Africa fit in in the global capitalist system? Why?

2. Distinguish disinvestment from divestment. Why have these proposed policies become important in the U.S. debate about apartheid?

3. What raised U.S. and European consciousness about apartheid in the 1980s and forced South African issues onto the political agendas in these countries?

4. What impact did Codes of Conduct have upon economic and political life in South Africa? Why were they adopted?

5. What are the goals of various political actors who seek to invoke economic sanctions against South Africa? How might these goals be sharpened and defined so that the effectiveness of sanctions may be measured?

CHAPTER FIVE

1. Why can we consider the South African regime as a pariah in world affairs? In what ways is it possible to isolate or reject a government for its political policies and yet continue to deal with it in cultural and economic terms?

2. Discuss the question of international organizations that are controlled by a group of states having limited power to enforce resolutions that they have easily passed. In the case of apartheid South Africa, how did these resolutions contribute to the weakening or fall of apartheid?

3. Describe the evolution of the Commonwealth of Nations and explain how changes in this organization over the years affected Pretoria's international role.

4. How have the actions of private citizens and nongovernmental organizations affected the international standing of South Africa? What sorts of groups appear to be the most influential and why?

5. If you were a member of the South African government, how would you advise your president to neutralize or reduce the effects of the following: a boycott of sporting ties; contributions from the World Council of Churches to South African human rights activists; decisions by a pension fund in Michigan for public workers to sell off their equity shares in corporations with facilities in South Africa? What are the potential gains and risks of your advice in each case?

6. Discuss the pros and cons of trying to change apartheid by either ending ties with South Africa or by actively engaging in South African affairs and thereby trying to challenge the regime there.

CHAPTER SIX

1. How accurate is the term "total onslaught" as it applies to South Africa's embattled situation in the world community?

2. By what techniques has Pretoria been able to evade the arms embargo of the United Nations? How effective have these evasions been?

3. Discuss the pros and cons of South African acquisition of nuclear weapons. What advantages and risks would they face should they secure such weapons?

4. To what extent has the so-called security establishment been involved in foreign and domestic policymaking in South Africa? Has this changed recently and, if so, under what circumstances?

CHAPTER SEVEN

1. To what degree would the changes that have been initiated in South Africa have been possible without pressures on Pretoria from abroad?

2. In considering the future of South Africa, outline a case in which racial and ethnic divisions in the country continue to bedevil its people. Why is it so difficult to transcend such exclusive social divisions? How might the international community, or parts thereof, help to decrease violence in that society?

3. Assuming that South Africa continues to make progress toward a future acceptable to the large majority of South Africans, how might the United States, for example, assist in the transition to majority rule?

4. Now that the cold war has been declared over, why should the United States expend its resources in trying to stabilize the polity in South Africa?

□ □ □

Notes

CHAPTER ONE

1. Francis Wilson and Mamphela Ramphele, *Uprooting Poverty: The South African Challenge* (New York: W. W. Norton, 1989).

2. The substance of this individual case is taken from *"We Will Not Move": The Struggle for Crossroads*, revised edition (London: International University Exchange Fund, 1978), p. 43.

3. As quoted in Pierre L. van den Berghe, *South Africa: A Study in Conflict* (Berkeley and Los Angeles: University of California Press, 1967), p. 118.

4. For background see Heribert Adam, *Modernizing Racial Domination: South Africa's Political Dynamics* (Berkeley and Los Angeles: University of California Press, 1971).

5. As quoted in the Cleveland *Plain Dealer*, November 17, 1989, p. 1A.

6. This section was drawn from Tom Lodge, *Black Politics in South Africa Since 1945* (London: Longman, 1983); Gail M. Gerhart, *Black Power in South Africa: The Evolution of an Ideology* (Berkeley: University of California Press, 1978); and Stephen M. Davis, *Apartheid's Rebels: Inside South Africa's Hidden War* (New Haven: Yale University Press, 1987).

7. See Gerhard Maré and Georgina Hamilton, *An Appetite for Power: Buthelezi's Inkatha and the Politics of "Loyal Resistance"* (Bloomington: Indiana University Press, 1987). A more sympathetic treatment is John Kane-Berman, "Inkatha: The Paradox of South African Politics," *Optima*, Vol. 30, No. 2 (February 1982), pp. 142–177.

8. George M. Frederickson, *White Supremacy: A Comparative Study of American and South African History* (New York and Oxford: Oxford University Press, 1981); and Stanley B. Greenberg, *Race and State in Capitalist Development: Comparative Perspectives* (New Haven and London: Yale University Press, 1980).

9. As quoted in the Cleveland *Plain Dealer*, December 15, 1986, p. 9A.

CHAPTER TWO

1. Amry Vandenbosch, *South Africa and the World: The Foreign Policy of Apartheid* (Lexington: University Press of Kentucky, 1970), p. 54.

2. Kenneth W. Grundy, "Intermediary Power and Global Dependency: The Case of South Africa," *International Studies Quarterly*, Vol. 20, No. 4 (December 1976), pp. 553–580.

3. South Africa, House of Assembly, *Debates (Hansard),* January 23–27, 1961, col. 98.

4. Quoted in James Barber and John Barratt, *South Africa's Foreign Policy: The Search for Status and Security, 1945–1988* (Cambridge: Cambridge University Press, 1990), p. 90.

5. J. E. Spence, "South Africa's Foreign Policy, The Evolution: 1945–1986," *Energos,* No. 14 (1986), pp. 5–16; and Barber and Barratt, *South Africa's Foreign Policy,* Part III.

6. Christopher Coker, *The United States and South Africa, 1968–1985: Constructive Engagement and Its Critics* (Durham, N.C.: Duke University Press, 1986).

7. Mohamed A. El-Khawas and Barry Cohen (eds.), *The Kissinger Study of Southern Africa: National Security Study Memorandum 39 (Secret)* (Westport, Conn.: Lawrence Hill and Co., 1976), pp. 105–106.

8. Coker, *The United States and South Africa;* and Pauline H. Baker, *The United States and South Africa: The Reagan Years* (New York: Ford Foundation–Foreign Policy Study Association, 1989).

9. M. J. Holland and Jean Monnet, "The European Community's Policy Towards South Africa: 12 Into One Won't Go," *Energos,* No. 14 (1986), pp. 41–49; and Janice Love, "The Potential Impact of Economic Sanctions Against South Africa," *Journal of Modern African Studies,* Vol. 26, No. 1 (April 1988).

10. See The Commonwealth Group of Eminent Persons, *Mission to South Africa: The Commonwealth Report* (Harmondsworth: Penguin Books, 1986).

11. Quoted in *Eastern Province Herald* (East London), June 30, 1989, p. 2; and in *Sunday Times* (Johannesburg), July 9, 1989, p. 24.

CHAPTER THREE

1. Quoted in John Dugard, *Human Rights and the South African Legal Order* (Princeton: Princeton University Press, 1978), p. 47.

2. This argument regarding South Africa was presented to the eleventh session of the UN General Assembly by Foreign Minister Eric H. Louw on November 15, 1956. See E. H. Louw, *The Case for South Africa* (New York: Macfadden Books, 1963), pp. 21–32; and C.A.W. Manning, "South Africa's Racial Policies—A Threat to Peace?" in N. J. Rhoodie (ed.), *South Africa Dialogue: Contrasts in South African Thinking on Basic Race Issues* (Johannesburg: McGraw-Hill, 1972), pp. 590–611.

3. Louw, *The Case for South Africa,* pp. 96–132.

4. See David L. Johnson, "Sanctions and South Africa," *Harvard International Law Journal,* Vol. 19 (1978), pp. 887–930.

5. I. William Zartman, *Ripe for Resolution: Conflict and Intervention in Africa* (New York and Oxford: Oxford University Press, 1989, updated edition).

CHAPTER FOUR

1. For a more complete exposition of this argument, see Kenneth W. Grundy, "Intermediary Power and Global Dependency: The Case of South Africa,"

International Studies Quarterly, Vol. 20, No. 4 (December 1976), pp. 553–580. See also Alf Stadler, *The Political Economy of Modern South Africa* (London: Croom Helm, 1987).

2. A useful bibliographical tool is *Pressure on Pretoria: Sanctions, Boycotts and the Divestment/Disinvestment Issue, 1964–1988,* compiled by Jacqueline A. Kalley (Johannesburg: South African Institute of International Affairs, 1988).

3. Ann and Neva Seidman, *South Africa and U.S. Multinational Corporations* (Westport, Conn.: Lawrence Hill and Co., 1977), p. 8.

4. Mark Orkin, *Disinvestment, the Struggle, and the Future: What Black South Africans Really Think* (Johannesburg: Ravan Press, 1986).

5. See Janice Love, *The U.S. Anti-Apartheid Movement: Local Activism in Global Politics* (New York: Praeger, 1985).

6. See *Weekly Mail* (Johannesburg), October 24–30, 1986, p. 13.

7. United States, General Accounting Office, Report to Congress, *South Africa: Trends in Trade, Lending and Investment* (Washington, D.C.: Government Printing Office, 1988), p. 28.

8. Ibid., p. 25.

9. *Weekly Mail,* March 17–23, 1989, p. 16.

10. Quoted in Anthony Sampson, "18 Days: A South African Journal," *New York Times Magazine,* March 18, 1990, pp. 40, 44.

11. James Barber, "Economic Sanctions as a Policy Instrument," *International Affairs,* Vol. 55, No. 3 (July 1979), pp. 367–384; Margaret P. Doxey, *Economic Sanctions and Economic Enforcement* (London: Macmillan, 1980); Richard C. Porter, "International Trade and Investment Sanctions: Potential Impact on the South African Economy," *Journal of Conflict Resolution,* Vol. 23, No. 4 (December 1979), pp. 579–612; David F. Gordon, "The Politics of International Sanctions: A Case Study of South Africa," in Miroslav Nincic and Peter Wallensteen (eds.), *Dilemmas of Economic Coercion: Sanctions in World Politics* (New York: Praeger, 1983), pp. 183–210; and the most comprehensive study of the South African case, Merle Lipton, *Sanctions and South Africa: The Dynamics of Economic Isolation* (London: Economist Intelligence Unit, 1988), Special Report No. 1119.

12. Johann Galtung, "On the Effects of International Economic Sanctions: With Examples from the Case of Rhodesia," *World Politics,* Vol. 19, No. 3 (April 1967), pp. 378–416; and Margaret P. Doxey, "The Rhodesian Sanctions Experiment," *Yearbook of World Affairs,* Vol. 25 (1971), pp. 142–162.

13. A complete list of economic actions against South Africa can be found in *South African Sanctions Directory, 1946–1988: Actions by Governments, Banks, Churches, Trade Unions, Universities, International and Regional Organizations,* compiled by Elna Schoeman (Johannesburg: South African Institute of International Affairs, 1988).

14. *Africa News* (Durham), Vol. 32, Nos. 1–2 (August 1989), pp. 9–13.

15. See "Sanctions and Exports," *Financial Mail* (Johannesburg), Vol. 102, Nos. 9–11 (November 28, 1986, and December 5 and 12, 1986).

16. *Sunday Star* (Johannesburg), December 28, 1986; *The Guardian* (London), March 27, 1984; and *The Observer* (London), August 5, 1984. Some of the techniques used to evade weapons sanctions can also be assumed to be employed

regarding economic sanctions. In this connection, see Signe Langren, *Embargo Disimplemented: South Africa's Military Industry* (New York: Oxford University Press, 1989).

17. Arthur Jay Klinghoffer, *Oiling the Wheels of Apartheid: Exposing South Africa's Secret Oil Trade* (Boulder, Colo.: Lynne Rienner, 1989).

18. *Weekly Mail*, August 4–10, 1989, p. 17.

19. *SA Report* (Johannesburg), November 10, 1989.

CHAPTER FIVE

1. Yehezkel Dror, *Crazy States: A Counterconventional Strategic Problem* (Lexington, Mass.: Heath Lexington, 1971).

2. See Robert E. Harkavy, "The Pariah State Syndrome," *Orbis*, Vol. 21, No. 3 (Fall 1977), pp. 623–649.

3. Richard Bissell, *Apartheid and International Organizations* (Boulder, Colo.: Westview Press, 1977).

4. See Abbott Alden et al., "The Decredentialization of South Africa," *Harvard International Law Journal*, Vol. 16 (1975), pp. 576–588.

5. Richard Bissell, "South Africa and International Ostracism," *World Affairs*, Vol. 137, No. 3 (Winter 1974–1975), p. 182.

6. See J.D.B. Miller, "South Africa's Departure," *Journal of Commonwealth Political Studies*, Vol. 1, No. 1 (November 1961), pp. 56–74; Amry Vandenbosch, *South Africa and the World: The Foreign Policy of Apartheid* (Lexington: University Press of Kentucky, 1970), pp. 174–188; and Ali A. Mazrui, *The Anglo-African Commonwealth: Political Friction and Cultural Fusion* (Oxford: Pergamon Press, 1967), pp. 27–41.

7. House of Assembly, *Debates (Hansard)*, March 29, 1962, cols. 3457 and 3452.

8. The Commonwealth Group of Eminent Persons, *Mission to South Africa: The Commonwealth Report* (Harmondsworth, England: Penguin, 1986).

9. Joan Brickhill, *Race Against Race: South Africa's 'Multinational' Sport Fraud* (London: International Defence and Aid Fund, 1976); and Richard E. Lapchick, *The Politics of Race and International Sport: The Case of South Africa* (Westport, Conn.: Greenwood, 1975).

10. See Peter Hain, *Don't Play with Apartheid: The Background to the Stop the Seventy Tour Campaign* (London: George Allen & Unwin, 1971).

11. *The Times* (London), May 18, 1987.

12. For further details on religious organizations, see Ann McKinstry Micou, *U.S. Church-Related Funding for Changes in South Africa: An Analysis and an Inventory* (New York: Institute of International Education, 1989), South African Information Exchange, Working Paper No. 7.

13. Kenneth W. Grundy, *"We're Against Apartheid, But . . .": Dutch Policy Toward South Africa* (Denver: University of Denver, 1974), Center on International Race Relations, Graduate School of International Studies, Studies in Race and Nations, Vol. 5, No. 3 (1973–1974).

14. The most complete coverage so far of this trend is Deon Geldenhuys, "South Africa: From International Isolation to Reintegration," a paper presented at the 32nd annual convention of the International Studies Association, Vancouver, Canada, March 22, 1991.

15. Senator J. William Fulbright makes this case well in *The Arrogance of Power* (New York: Random House, 1967).

CHAPTER SIX

1. Republic of South Africa, Department of Defence, *White Paper on Defence and Armaments Supply, 1982* (Cape Town: South African Navy Printing and Photographic Unit, 1982), p. 2.

2. House of Assembly, *Debates (Hansard)*, January 31, 1978, cols. 103–104.

3. Ibid., January 28, 1981, cols. 235–236.

4. Signe Landgren, *Embargo Disimplemented: South Africa's Military Industry* (New York: Oxford University Press, 1989), especially pp. 231–241.

5. Robert S. Jaster, "Pretoria's Nuclear Diplomacy," *CSIS Africa Notes*, No. 81 (January 22, 1988); and J.D.L. Moore, *South Africa and Nuclear Proliferation: South Africa's Nuclear Capabilities and Intentions in the Context of International Non-Proliferation Policies* (New York: St. Martin's Press, 1987).

6. The controversy regarding South Africa's alleged collaboration with Israel in weapons development is covered in James Adams, *The Unnatural Alliance* (London: Quartet Books, 1984); Robert E. Harkavy, "Pariah States and Nuclear Proliferation," *International Organization*, Vol. 35, No. 1 (Winter 1981); and Peter L. Bunce, "The Growth of South Africa's Defence Industry and Its Israeli Connection," *Journal of the Royal United Services Institute for Defence Studies*, Vol. 129 (June 1984).

7. These operations are well documented and analyzed in Joseph Hanlon, *Beggar Your Neighbours: Apartheid Power in Southern Africa* (London: James Currey, 1986); Robert S. Jaster, *South Africa and Its Neighbours: The Dynamics of Regional Conflict*, Adelphi Paper 209 (London: International Institute for Strategic Studies, Summer 1986); Kenneth W. Grundy, *The Militarization of South African Politics* (Oxford: Oxford University Press, 1988); and Phyllis Johnson and David Martin, *Apartheid Terrorism: The Destabilization Report* (London: James Currey, in association with the Commonwealth Secretariat, 1989).

8. For evidence of continued assistance to Renamo, see Johnson and Martin, *Apartheid Terrorism*, pp. 23–31. The most detached coverage of Renamo is Tom Young, "The MNR/RENAMO: External and Internal Dynamics," *African Affairs*, Vol. 89, No. 357 (October 1990), pp. 491–509.

□ □ □

Suggested Readings

Adam, Heribert. *Modernizing Racial Domination: The Dynamics of South African Politics.* Berkeley: University of California Press, 1971.

Adam, Heribert, and Kogila Moodley. *South Africa Without Apartheid: Dismantling Racial Domination.* Berkeley: University of California Press, 1986.

Baker, Pauline H. *The United States and South Africa: The Reagan Years.* New York: Ford Foundation–Foreign Policy Association, 1989.

Barber, James, and John Barratt. *South Africa's Foreign Policy: The Search for Status and Security, 1945–1988.* Cambridge: Cambridge University Press, 1990.

Berridge, Geoff. *Economic Power in Anglo-South African Diplomacy: Simonstown, Sharpeville and After.* Atlantic Highlands, N.J.: Humanities Press, 1981.

Cock, Jacklyn, and Laurie Nathan (eds.). *War and Society: The Militarization of South Africa.* New York: St. Martin's Press, 1989.

Coker, Christopher. *The United States and South Africa, 1968–1985: Constructive Engagement and Its Critics.* Durham, N.C.: Duke University Press, 1986.

Commonwealth Committee of Foreign Ministers on South Africa. *South Africa: The Sanctions Report.* Harmondsworth, England: Penguin, 1989.

Davis, Stephen M. *Apartheid's Rebels: Inside South Africa's Hidden War.* New Haven: Yale University Press, 1987.

El-Khawas, Mohamed A., and Barry Cohen (eds.). *The Kissinger Study of Southern Africa: National Security Study Memorandum (Secret).* Westport, Conn: Lawrence Hill & Co., 1976.

Foreign Policy Study Foundation, Inc. *South Africa: Time Running Out.* Berkeley: University of California Press, Report of the Study Commission on U.S. Policy Toward Southern Africa, 1981.

Frederickson, George M. *White Supremacy: A Comparative Study of American and South African History.* New York: Oxford University Press, 1981.

Geldenhuys, Deon. *The Diplomacy of Isolation: South African Foreign Policy Making.* Johannesburg: Macmillan South Africa, 1984.

Gerhart, Gail M. *Black Power in South Africa: The Evolution of an Ideology.* Berkeley: University of California Press, 1978.

Giliomee, Hermann, and Lawrence Schlemmer (eds.). *Up Against the Fences: Poverty, Passes and Privilege in South Africa.* New York: St. Martin's Press, 1985.

————— . *Negotiating South Africa's Future* London: Macmillan, 1989.

Greenberg, Stanley B. *Legitimating the Illegitimate: State, Markets and Resistance in South Africa.* Berkeley: University of California Press, 1987.

————. *Race and State in Capitalist Development: Comparative Perspectives.* New Haven: Yale University Press, 1980.

Grundy, Kenneth W. *The Militarization of South African Politics.* Oxford: Oxford University Press, 1988.

Hanlon, Joseph, and Roger Ormond. *The Sanctions Handbook.* Harmondsworth, England: Penguin, 1987.

Holland, Martin. *The European Community and South Africa: European Political Co-operation Under Strain.* London: Pinter, 1988.

Jackson, Richard A. (ed.). *The Multinational Corporation and Social Policy: Special Reference to General Motors in South Africa.* New York: Praeger, 1974.

Johnson, Phyllis, and David Martin. *Apartheid Terrorism: The Destabilization Report.* Bloomington: Indiana University Press, 1989.

Johnson, R. W. *How Long Will South Africa Survive?* New York: Oxford University Press, 1977.

Kahn, Haidu Ali. *The Political Economy of Sanctions Against Apartheid.* Boulder, Colo.: Lynne Rienner, 1989.

Klinghoffer, Arthur Jay. *Oiling the Wheels of Apartheid: Exploring South Africa's Secret Oil Trade.* Boulder, Colo.: Lynne Rienner, 1989.

Landgren, Signe. *Embargo Disimplemented: South Africa's Military Industry.* Oxford: Oxford University Press, 1989.

Lewis, Stephen R. *The Economics of Apartheid.* New York: Council on Foreign Relations Press, 1989.

Lodge, Tom. *Black Politics in South Africa since 1945.* London: Longman, 1983.

Love, Janice. *The U.S. Anti-Apartheid Movement: Local Activism in Global Politics.* New York: Praeger, 1985.

Minter, William. *King Solomon's Mines: Western Interests and the Burdened History of Southern Africa.* New York: Basic Books, 1986.

Moore, J.D.L. *South Africa and Nuclear Proliferation: South Africa's Nuclear Capabilities and Intentions in the Context of International Non-Proliferation Policies.* New York: St. Martin's Press, 1987.

Orkin, Mark. *Disinvestment, the Struggle, and the Future: What Black South Africans Really Think.* Johannesburg: Ravan Press, 1986.

Rogaly, Gail Linda (compiler). *South Africa's Foreign Relations, 1961–1979: A Select and Partially Annotated Bibliography.* Johannesburg: South African Institute of International Affairs, Bibliographical series No. 7, 1980.

Schmidt, Elizabeth. *Decoding Corporate Camouflage: U.S. Business Support for Apartheid.* Washington: Institute for Policy Studies, 1980.

Schoeman, Elna (compiler). *South African Sanctions Directory, 1946–1988: Actions by Governments, Banks, Churches, Trade Unions, Universities, International and Regional Organizations.* Johannesburg: South African Institute of International Affairs, Bibliographical series No. 18, 1988.

Seidman, Ann, and Neva Seidman. *South Africa and U.S. Multinational Corporations.* Westport, Conn: Lawrence Hill & Co., 1977.

Sincere, Richard E., Jr. *The Politics of Sentiment: Churches and Foreign Investment in South Africa.* Lanham, Md.: Ethics and Public Policy Center, 1984.

Stadler, Alf. *The Political Economy of Modern South Africa.* London: Croom Helm, 1987.

Vandenbosch, Amry. *South Africa and the World: The Foreign Policy of Apartheid.* Lexington: University Press of Kentucky, 1970.

Wilson, Francis, and Mamphela Ramphele. *Uprooting Poverty: The South African Challenge.* New York: W. W. Norton, 1989.

□ □ □

Glossary

African National Congress was founded in 1912 and is currently the most popular voice for a nonracial, majoritarian, unitary South Africa.

Afrikaners constitute the dominant white population group. They are descendents of Dutch and French Huguenot settlers, many of whom arrived in South Africa in or soon after 1652; and they speak Afrikaans, a language based on Dutch.

Armscor, the Armaments Corporation of South Africa, is a parastatal corporation that coordinates armaments production to offset the impact of the UN arms embargo against South Africa.

Bantustans. See **Homelands.**

Black Consciousness Movement is an outgrowth of the South African Students' Organization, headed by Steven Biko. It came into vogue in the 1970s and sought to develop and publicize a coherent ideology of Black Consciousness and cultural nationalism.

Charterists are those who subscribe to the Freedom Charter of 1955, as opposed to the Africanists, who advocate racial identity and self-expression. Most of the Congress movements are regarded as Charterist, whereas the Black Consciousness and Azanian groups tend to be Africanist.

"Constructive engagement," the shorthand rubric for U.S. policy toward South Africa during the Reagan years, called for greater interaction with South African government organs in order to encourage them to reform. Its critics regarded "constructive engagement" as a tilt toward the apartheid regime rather than as an even-handed policy.

Destabilization was the military and economic policy of Pretoria toward neighboring states in the 1970s and 1980s, when efforts were made to weaken governments and economies that were hostile to South Africa or that were providing sanctuary to SWAPO and the ANC.

Disinvestment is the closure or sale by a foreign company of its South African operations in order to withdraw and repatriate its assets.

Divestment refers to the sale of shares of stock in a company because that company does business in South Africa or does it in an unsatisfactory manner.

Freedom Charter is a statement of goals adopted in 1955 by the Congress of the People (including the ANC), stating African aspirations for a nonracial, egalitarian state.

Group Areas Act is the 1950 legislation by which all urban areas of South Africa are divided into zones in which members of one race and only one race

151

may reside, go to school, or conduct business. Throughout the 1980s, numerous exceptions were instituted, but the fundamentals of the law are still in force. This act is regarded as one of the legal pillars of apartheid. In February 1991, State President de Klerk proposed to repeal it.

Homelands are the territorial subdivisions created by the apartheid government and reserved for various tribal groups; they are popularly known as **Bantustans.** At present, four homelands have been granted ostensible independence, and five have various degrees of internal self-government.

Inkatha is the political movement of the Zulu people, headed by Chief Mangosuthu Buthelezi of the KwaZulu homeland.

Mass Democratic Movement is an informal collection of progressive anti-apartheid organizations. For a short time in the 1980s, it replaced the banned United Democratic Front.

Multinational corporations are business enterprises based in one country and yet doing business (largely manufacturing, service, or extraction) in other countries by means of direct investment.

National Party, the ruling party since 1948, is generally identified with the Afrikaners, although in 1990 it announced that the NP would be open to all South Africans, regardless of race.

National Security Management System was the elaborate, many-layered security network dominated by the SADF. It was created in 1986 and replaced by the National Coordinating Mechanism in 1989.

National Security Study Memorandum 39 is a secret position paper prepared by the U.S. National Security Council in 1969 under the direction of Henry Kissinger. It defines alleged U.S. interests in southern Africa, and its Option No. 2 appears to have been adopted as U.S. policy, thereby tilting the Nixon administration toward further dealings with Pretoria.

Newly industrialized countries are Third World states that have managed to realize rapid growth in manufacturing and exports by virtue of an inexpensive but hard working and well-trained work force (e.g., Taiwan, Hong Kong, Mexico, and Brazil).

Non-Proliferation Treaty of 1968 was an effort by the nuclear powers to limit the spread of nuclear weapons to those powers that already have them. As of 1988, 128 nonnuclear states were party to the treaty. South Africa was not a signatory.

Organization of African Unity is an intergovernmental organization of states in Africa created in 1963. (South Africa has thus far been excluded.)

Pan-Africanist Congress was founded in 1959 as a breakaway from the ANC. It was declared illegal in 1960 and its leaders were arrested. Unbanned in 1990, it currently takes a radical position in opposition to negotiating with government.

Population Registration Act of 1950 required the registration of all individuals by race in order to make prohibitions against race-mixing enforceable. In 1991 legislation was introduced in parliament to repeal it.

Renamo, which stands for Resistençia Naçional Moçambicana, was created by the Rhodesian Central Intelligence Organization and then sustained by the

SADF's Military Intelligence. Sometimes known by the acronym MNR, it has been involved in actively destabilizing the Frelimo government and the Mozambican countryside.

Sanctions are deliberate actions intended to inflict deprivation on a target state, government, or people through the limitation or cessation of customary relations. Most often, sanctions are invoked by governments and cover economic means; but private groups sometimes seek to deprive targets of relations, and occasionally political, military, legal, and other means are employed.

Sharpeville is the scene of the 1960 massacre of some seventy Blacks who had marched on the local police station in order to turn in their passbooks. The government responded by clamping down on Black opposition and banning both the ANC and the PAC.

Soweto, the South Western Townships outside of Johannesburg, is home for some 2 million Blacks. The Soweto uprising in 1976 launched a three-month period of intense violence, perpetrated mostly by the SAP against township school children, that (officially) accounted for nearly 600 deaths.

Sullivan Principles constitute the code of conduct for U.S. firms operating in South Africa. Developed by Reverend Leon Sullivan of the General Motors Board of Directors in 1977, they have fallen into disuse since the adoption of the Comprehensive Anti-Apartheid Act of 1986.

SWAPO, the South West African People's Organization, is the major nationalist independence movement in Namibia and the ruling party in Namibia since independence in 1990.

"Total onslaught" is the term used among the ruling elite in South Africa to describe the multi-faceted resistance to apartheid and to minority government. Coined by thinkers in the SADF it has been downplayed since 1985 or so. The "total national strategy" to oppose the onslaught was very much in vogue throughout the P. W. Botha years, however.

Umkhonto we Sizwe, sometimes known as MK, is the armed force of the ANC. It was created after the ANC was banned in 1960. Generally, MK was quiescent after the 1963 terrorism trial at Rivonia, but new life was breathed into it after 1983.

UNITA, or União Nacional para la Independência Total de Angola, is one of the major movements opposing the Angolan government. Until 1989, UNITA was supported militarily by South Africa and still gets assistance from the United States.

United Democratic Front was an umbrella organization that consisted of more than 600 national and local groups committed to the defeat of apartheid. Established for the purpose of coordinating protest activities against the 1983 constitutional referendum, it continued until 1991, despite the banning of many of its component groups and the detention of its top leadership.

□ □ □

Chronology

A.D.	Bantu-speaking peoples settle in what is now South Africa, although they have been preceded for centuries by ancestors of the San and Khoi peoples.
1652–1795	The Dutch East India Company establishes a replenishing station on the Cape. Dutch, and later French Huguenots and Germans, settle the Cape. The indigenous population of San and Khoi peoples either dies off, or is killed, chased inland, or in some cases assimilated. Their land and cattle are stolen. Slaves from the East Indies, Madagascar, and elsewhere in Africa are imported.
1795–1806	The British seize the Cape from the Dutch.
1816–1828	Shaka consolidates the Zulu kingdom and launches wars against neighboring peoples.
1820	Several thousand British settlers arrive in the eastern Cape. Frontier wars against the Xhosa last into the late 1870s.
1836–1840	The "Great Trek" of Afrikaner farmers into the interior occurs. They flee British rule.
1838	The Battle of Blood River (Natal), at which Afrikaners defeat the Zulu.
1843	Britain annexes Natal.
1860–1911	The British import indentured laborers from India to work in Natal sugar cane fields.
1867	Diamonds are discovered near Kimberley in the northern Cape.
1877	Britain annexes Transvaal (an Afrikaner republic).
1880–1881	The First Anglo-Boer War, in which the Afrikaners regain their independence.
1886	Gold is discovered on the Witwatersrand in Transvaal.
1899–1902	The Second Anglo-Boer War, in which the British are victorious. The once independent republics of the Transvaal and the Orange Free State become self-governing crown colonies. Great enmity between Afrikaners and the British grows out of the harsh policies toward Afrikaner civilians.
1910	The Union of South Africa is created as a self-governing British dominion. Its all-white, Afrikaner-dominated government and all-white parliament begin to codify segregationist laws for the entire country.

1912	The South African Native National Congress is founded and in 1923 is renamed the African National Congress (ANC).
1914	The National Party is founded to counter a government that many Afrikaners feel is too subservient to Great Britain.
1915	South Africa occupies South-West Africa (Namibia), a German colony, and in 1920 is granted a League of Nations mandate to govern the territory.
1921	The South African Communist Party is formed, originally largely a white workers party.
1936	The Natives Trust and Land Act increases the land set aside for African reserves from about 7 percent to 13.7 percent of all land.
1939	South Africa decides, by a narrow parliamentary majority, to enter World War II on the side of Great Britain. The decision divides the whites, and many Afrikaners sympathize with Nazi Germany. Activists are incarcerated. General Smuts becomes a prominent Allied leader.
1948	The National Party, led by Daniel Malan, wins a narrow electoral victory and begins to enact "apartheid" policies by which long-standing policies of racial segregation are codified and enlarged, and new segregationist schemes are instituted.
1949	The ANC adopts an active program of nonviolent protest and disobedience.
1950	The Population Registration Act, Group Areas Act, Immorality Act, Suppression of Communism Act are passed.
1951	The Bantu Authorities Act is passed.
1952	The Defiance Campaign is organized by the ANC. Nonviolent civil disobedience leads to the jailing of some 8,500 protesters.
1953	The Bantu Education Act and Public Safety Act are passed.
1955	The Freedom Charter is drafted at the Congress of the People by an alliance of the ANC and Indian, Coloured, and White organizations.
1956	Widespread protests lead to the arrests and trials of prominent ANC leaders, including ANC president Chief Albert Luthuli and Nelson Mandela.
1958	The theorist of apartheid, Dr. Hendrik Verwoerd, becomes prime minister.
1959	The Pan-Africanist Congress (PAC) is formed by "Africanists" opposed to prominent roles for non-Africans in the ANC. The promotion of the Bantu Self-Government Act establishes that all Africans will eventually become citizens of one of eight ethnic "national units" (homelands) that will eventually gain their independence from South Africa.
1960	The Sharpeville massacre, in which more than 70 unarmed protesters are shot and killed as they demonstrate against the pass laws. A state of emergency follows and nearly 2,000 ANC

and PAC activists are arrested. Both the PAC and the ANC are outlawed as a result.

1961 The ANC abandons the policy of nonviolence, and its armed wing, *Umkhonto we Sizwe,* launches an ineffectual sabotage campaign. South Africa leaves the Commonwealth under pressure, and South Africa's white voters narrowly decide to become a republic.

1962–1967 A variety of security laws are passed to enable authorities to crush African resistance to apartheid.

1964 Eight ANC leaders are sentenced to life imprisonment, including Mandela, Sisulu, and Mbeki.

1966 Prime Minister Verwoerd is assassinated; John Vorster becomes prime minister.

1968 The South African Students Organization and the Black People's Convention are founded. Black consciousness gets a popular footing. Meanwhile, multiracial political parties are outlawed and Coloured representation (by whites) is ended in the white parliament.

1974 Junior officers in Portugal overthrow the Caetano regime in Lisbon and pledge to end the colonial wars in Angola, Mozambique, and Guinee (Bissau). The UN General Assembly suspends the credentials of the South African delegation, thereby denying South African participation in the General Assembly.

1975 Mozambique becomes independent in June, Angola in November.

1976 The Soweto uprising, in which at first student protests and then more generalized ones spread throughout the country. Police and military forces fire on demonstrators, resulting in an estimated 1,000 deaths. Eventually the protests are repressed.

1977 Steve Biko is murdered while in police detention. A number of black-consciousness and resistance movements are banned. The UN follows with a mandatory arms embargo against South Africa.

1978 Vorster resigns after a scandal and he is replaced as prime minister by P. W. Botha. The UN Security Council adopts Resolution 435 calling for a transition to independence sponsored and administered by the UN.

1980 Zimbabwe gains independence. Students boycott schools for nine months. The ANC launches a sabotage campaign designed for maximum propaganda effect.

1981 Authorities begin harassing and "endorsing out" squatters from "Crossroads," outside of Cape Town.

1982 The General Assembly proclaims 1982 as the International Year of Mobilization of Sanctions Against South Africa.

1983 The United Democratic Front (UDF) is formed among progressive organizations supportive of the principles expressed in the Freedom Charter. By constitutional referendum, whites adopt a tricameral parliament divided by race. Black Africans have no official role in this change, but massive protests lead into wider unrest.

1984   Organized township resistance leads the government to mobilize. South Africa signs the Nkomati Accord with Mozambique by which the two parties agree to cease their support of movements based in their territories that seek to overthrow the other government.

1985   A state of emergency is imposed in certain magisterial districts. Violent deaths mount into the hundreds. Foreign banks suspend credit to South Africa. President Reagan imposes limited trade and financial sanctions in an effort to preempt more stringent U.S. Congressional sanctions.

1986   The South African Defense Force attacks alleged ANC bases in neighboring countries, thereby undermining the mission of the Commonwealth's Eminent Persons Group to seek a formula for transition to majority rule. The state of emergency is widened to include the entire country. The U.S. Congress overrides the presidential veto to enact the Comprehensive Anti-Apartheid Act.

1987   Although the government appears to be regaining the upper hand against organized resistance, violence continues, increasing especially between various Black parties and their followers.

1988   The government bans a number of antiapartheid organizations, including the UDF. Negotiations on Namibian independence gain momentum under the guidance of the United States and the Soviet Union. In December, agreements are signed stating that the independence process there will commence April 1, 1989, and end in 1990.

1989   F. W. de Klerk replaces Botha as state president, and a number of security measures are suspended or relaxed. Optimism grows as reforms are instituted.

1990   In February, resistance movements are unbanned and Mandela is released from prison. Namibia is granted its independence. Mandela makes several major tours to Europe, Africa, and North America. De Klerk travels, symbolizing South Africa's growing acceptance by the world community. The government begins "talks about talks" with the ANC, and in August the ANC suspends the armed struggle. Nonetheless, violence increases in intensity, especially between ANC and Inkatha supporters, first in Natal and later on the Rand. More than 6,000 people are killed in 1990 and the beginning of 1991.

1991   De Klerk introduces into parliament measures to repeal the Land Acts, Group Areas Act, and Population Registration Act. Buthelezi and Mandela meet amid continuing violence.

□ □ □

About the Book and Author

South Africa conjures up many images in the international consciousness: Nelson Mandela on a triumphant world tour; riots and violence in black villages; an alternatively defensive and smug white ruling class resisting what is probably inevitable change. Why should a single country, remote from the world's centers of economic and military power, command such intense international interest? How does the way in which a country runs its government become an international issue dominating human rights agendas the world over?

The answers may be found in a single word—apartheid—perhaps the most visible if not the most pervasive or violent form of undemocratic governance in the international system. In this concise and balanced overview, Kenneth Grundy explains the theory and practice of apartheid, puts it in historical context, and shows how individuals, groups, and governments seek to address its implications. In the process, he examines South Africa's role in the world's political economy; the nature of diplomatic, economic, and military pressures aimed at the government in Pretoria; and the range of policy options facing the Western world as it seeks to end apartheid while preserving South Africa's productivity, stability, and sovereignty. The roles of sanctions, disinvestment, and arms embargoes are given particular attention.

Written for students of all levels in international relations, foreign policy, and area studies, *South Africa: Domestic Crisis and Global Challenge* includes maps, discussion questions, suggested readings, and a glossary.

Kenneth W. Grundy is the Marcus A. Hanna Professor of Political Science at Case Western Reserve University and the author of six books, including *The Militarization of South African Politics* and *Soldiers Without Politics: Blacks in the South African Armed Forces*. In addition, he regularly contributes commentary on international relations to various newspapers. He has taught and done extended research in South Africa, England, Zambia, Uganda, the Netherlands, and Ireland.

□ □ □

Index

Africa, 28, 29, 32, 43, 81
  Black-ruled, 31, 32, 82, 94, 117,
    133. *See also individual countries*
  independent states in (1956–1965),
    31
  See also Southern Africa; *under*
    Soviet Union
African National Congress (ANC)
    (1912), 12–13, 14, 15, 16, 18, 19,
    31, 38, 61, 72, 95, 98–99, 117,
    118, 123, 125, 133
  banned (1960), 14, 29
  and CYL, 13
  in exile, 16
  factions, 14, 128
  and Inkatha party, 17, 18
  mass protests (1952), 14
  in Mozambique, 35
  and NP, 131
  police informers in, 14
  and popular support, 15, 128
  sabotage campaign, 15, 30, 35
  and SACP, 13, 18
  and socialist bloc, 47
  in Southern African states, 35, 37,
    113
  unbanned (1990), 17, 121
African nationalism, 9, 13, 31, 33, 54
Afrikaans (language), 15
Afrikaners, 7, 8, 26, 54, 64, 80
  nationalists, 81
  right-wing, 18, 121, 126
Afrikaner Weerstandsbeweging
    (AWB), 121, 126
Aircraft, 109, 110
All-African Council of Churches, 86,
    91

American Committee on Africa, 59
American Friends Service
    Committee, 59
Amin, Idi, 76
Amnesty International, 92
ANC. *See* African National Congress
Anglo-American Corporation, 72
Anglo-Boer War (1899–1902), 81
Angola, 20, 33, 117, 127, 130, 133
  armed struggle (1961–1974), 31,
    48, 49, 112
  and Cuba, 48, 49
  hunger, 114
  independence (1975), 113, 118
  Marxist government, 47
  oil exports, 48
  radar system, 49
  and South Africa, 34–35, 49, 50,
    109, 112, 113, 114, 115, 116, 119,
    120, 124
  and Soviet Union, 47, 115
  See also under United States
Antarctic Treaty (1959), 80
Antiapartheid movements, 85–86, 93,
    94
  unbanned (1990), 121, 128, 131
Anticolonialism, 27
Antiimperialism, 9, 52, 53
Antipass protest (1960), 14, 29
Apartheid (1948), 8, 19, 21, 24, 28,
    29, 77, 103, 114, 117
  Black agents of, 36, 121
  and change, 11–12, 17, 18, 21, 24,
    34, 37–38, 39–40, 44, 63–64,
    66–67, 89, 99–100, 101, 122,
    123, 133–134
  costs, 126